The Growing Tree

The Growing Tree

Revised Edition

Brayton F. Wilson

THE UNIVERSITY OF MASSACHUSETTS PRESS   AMHERST

Copyright © 1984 by
The University of Massachusetts Press
Second paperback printing, 1988
All rights reserved
Printed in the United States of America
L C 84–3577
I S B N 0–87023–423–4 cloth; 424–2 paper
Library of Congress Cataloging in Publication Data
appear on the last printed page of this book.

To Norm Lake

Contents

Illustrations

The objective of this book has not changed since the first edition. It is intended for people who want to know how trees grow. Although I have rewritten and updated the whole book, much of the content is basically the same. I have emphasized more strongly how to look at a tree as a growing, integral system. A few chapters have been omitted and a few have been added to reflect my changing interests over the fifteen years since the first edition. With all these changes it is really a new and different book, not just a second edition. Various material on growth regulation, which had been scattered through the book, has been collected into a separate chapter. Major virtues of the first edition were that it was short and comprehensible. I hope these characteristics hold true in the revised edition.

1 : What is a tree and how does it grow?

MOST PEOPLE HAVE an intuitive sense of what a tree is. They visualize a tall, single-stemmed, woody plant with a branched crown and many leaves. This tree form, or design, is common to many otherwise unrelated plant genera and families. Trees can compete with other plants because they specialize in becoming the tallest, longest-living plants. This competitive ability is presumably why the tree form has arisen in so many plant groups. Developing a precise definition of a tree is difficult and unrewarding. It probably is worthwhile to point out some plant forms that are not considered in this book. Palms and tree ferns meet many of the qualifications of trees, but they are not really woody, most do not branch, and they generally have only a few, large leaves. Shrub species may grow like trees, but usually they are relatively short and have multiple stems at the base. On the other hand, tree seedlings do not meet the qualifications of trees because they are too small and unbranched, but they will ultimately become trees and have to be considered when discussing tree growth. Individuals of tree species may not grow to be trees under extremes like mountain-top environments or the severe treatment accorded them as bonsai specimens, but they are still trees. There are exceptions and borderline cases that muddy any attempt to classify organisms, and trees are no exception. Yet, the concept of a tree form is useful and trees in general have some special growth characteristics and limitations that merit discussion separate from the multitude of other plant forms.

People know trees, like them, and value them, but trees are so

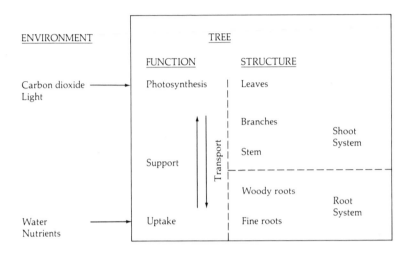

1   TREE AS A SYSTEM
Diagrammatic model of the relation between a tree and its environment.

big and apparently so hopelessly complicated that it may seem impossible to understand how they grow. The aim of this book is to show how the great size and the incredible complexity of a tree is generated by relatively few processes, repeated over and over each year as the tree grows. H. M. Ward wrote "what a complex matter in its summation, but what a simple one in its graduated steps, the shaping of a tree is."[1] His statement is just as true now as it was when he made it in 1909. This first chapter will outline the approach of the rest of the book, which is, essentially, how the graduated steps of tree growth occur and how they are regulated.

We can view a complex tree as a simple system with relatively few types of structures (fig. 1). The leaves are the productive machines of the tree. They take carbon dioxide from the air, light energy from the sun, and some water from the soil and combine them in the process of photosynthesis to produce carbohydrates. Carbohydrates are the basic molecular components used to construct the mass of a tree. As carbon dioxide diffuses into the leaves from the air, water vapor inevitably diffuses out of the leaves to the air. Therefore, huge amounts of water are lost from the tree. The roots take in the nitrogen and minerals that are used with the carbohydrates from photosynthesis to synthesize the complex array of substances used in tree growth. The roots take in water needed to replace that lost from the leaves; they also anchor the tree in the ground. The shoot system (the stem and branches) serves the functions of supporting the leaves, of transporting water, minerals, and nitrogen to the leaves, and of transporting the materials made in the leaves, which we can lump together and call *photosynthate*, to the rest of the tree where they can be used for growth.

Looking at a tree as a system with only three components—leaves, shoot system, and root system—can be helpful in understanding how a tree works, but it certainly does not help explain why trees look the way they do. The look of trees results from their design as the tallest and longest-lived plants. Trees have not invented any new types of structures or processes that other plants do not have. They just have an incredible number of parts that are highly organized. They have refined some internal anatomy for physical strength and to allow physiological processes to proceed efficiently, but they have not created new processes.

The basic design of a tree is comparable to a tower bearing many small solar collectors. The objective of the design is to get lots of leaves high in the air, at low cost in photosynthate. The design must be strong enough to last for many years, perhaps centuries. Yet, trees cannot be overdesigned (extra strong) because that would be wasteful of valuable energy and materials that could be used in other parts of the structure. The trees discussed in this book have single, tall stems and many branches at the top. Some treelike plants, for example palm and tree ferns, have single, tall stems, but either they do not branch or they scarcely branch.

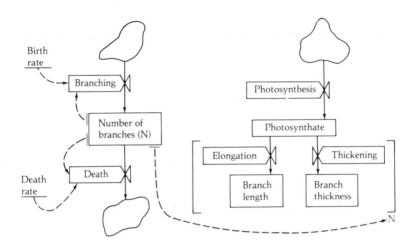

2   SHOOT-SYSTEM GROWTH
Relational diagram of levels and rates in shoot-system growth. On the
left is a population model for the number of branches (N); on the right
is a model for branch growth that is repeated N times (once for each
branch). Valve symbols are rate variables, boxes are level variables,
clouds are level variables outside the system as defined, underlined values are constants not affected by the system as defined.

In contrast to towers built by humans, trees are dynamic systems. They grow, and they can only grow using materials that
they produce themselves. A tree emerging from a germinating
seed starts as a tiny shoot and root system with enough stored
material for the very first growth. Small as this tiny tree is, it is
just as much a functional system as a large tree. In order to grow
after the stored material is used up, the tree must produce more
photosynthate than needed to maintain itself. As it grows the tree
constantly changes as the extra photosynthate is used in growth,
yet the tree always retains its integrity as a system. The various
parts (leaves, shoot system, and root system) are kept in balance
so that the tree operates efficiently.

Methods developed for analyzing dynamic systems are helpful

in understanding how trees grow.[2] At any one time a system can be described by a series of level or state variables (fig. 2). For example, a leafless tree in winter can be described by knowing the length and thickness of each branch. In addition, one must know some rules about the branching pattern—how the branches are connected and oriented. Knowing the level variables and the branching patterns it is possible to make a reasonable three-dimensional reconstruction of a tree. In any dynamic system the level variables change over time through the action of rate variables. In a tree the rate variables are growth variables (fig. 2). To continue the example above, after a year of growth each branch becomes longer and thicker because of the growth rate variables, i.e., elongation and thickening. There are additional rate variables that determine the number of branches. The change in number of branches in a tree can be modeled the same way any population is modeled. The rate of branching is the birth rate. It is a product of the number of preexisting parent branches and branch birth rate (the number of new branches each parent branch produces each year). The rate of branch death determines how many old branches are lost. It is the product of the probability of a branch dying and the number of old branches that might die.

The form or look of the tree arises from annually repeated patterns of branching, elongation, thickening, and death. The differences in form between fast- and slow-growing trees, or between trees of different species, result not from different processes but from different rates of the processes. Form is also determined by the characteristic orientation of branches to each other, and by any changes in orientation over time. The patterns that determine form result from differences in growth rates among branches and from the characteristic orientation of the branches. Changes in orientation are caused by bending of branches.

The development described so far has been gradual, orderly, and fairly predictable, but there can also be unpredictable events that affect tree form. Storms, frosts, insects, diseases, animals, and man can all kill or remove various parts of a tree to produce immediate structural changes. In general, the tree responds to such damage by changing growth in ways that tend to restore the original form. Thus, the system can, within limits, repair itself.

A model for the development of the root system would be nearly identical to that for the shoot system. There is a population of roots with a birth and a death rate. Each root elongates and thickens at some rate and differences among roots create patterns. Orientation does not change because the roots are supported in the soil.

The regulation of growth results from the regulation of the rates of the growth processes. After determining what levels and rates are important, the complex part of systems analysis is to figure out how rates are controlled. Each of the general processes that we have identified is really the sum of many processes at the cellular level as meristems produce cells that later differentiate into the various tissues of the tree. The rates are regulated by feedback controls from the amount of available growth factors (carbohydrates, etc.) that can be used to build new cells. Rates are also controlled by the level of growth regulators (hormones and inhibitors) at the site and by conditions within the meristem (temperature, water stress, etc.).

Most of the book will describe the processes of tree growth, the regulation of those processes, and some of the differences between trees. These characteristics determine the success of the individual tree as a tower design, but there are many other factors that determine the success of a tree species. An individual tree may be visualized as a population of roots and shoots. A species is a population of individual trees. Success of a species depends on the perpetuation and survival of the population, not on the survival of a particular individual. Survival of individual trees, the photosynthetic towers, is vital to the success of a tree species, but equally so is the survival through all the other stages of the life cycle. John Harper's statement that "a plant is only the means by which a seed produces more seeds"[3] puts the huge tower structure that we call a tree in the proper perspective from the point of view of species success. Enough individuals must survive to produce seed and the seed must be distributed and grow into new trees to produce more seed to perpetuate the species.

Despite the fact that production of seeds through sexual reproduction is such a key factor to survival of a species, the process will not be covered in this book except to discuss some examples where the process affects the form of a tree. Sexual reproduction is complex. It requires production of totally different types of plant organs to ultimately produce the male and female reproductive cells plus the specialized layers of the seed and fruit that surround the embryo of the new tree. In addition, pollination and fertilization must occur and the seed must be distributed to favorable sites for growth of the new tree. This fascinating subsystem of plant growth is so complicated that it merits far more detailed treatment than it receives in this book.[4]

THE TREE DESIGN has developed in a wide variety of plant groups. Many groups that have only herbaceous representatives in the temperate zones have tree forms, or treelike forms, in the tropics. F. Hallé, R. A. A. Oldeman, and P. B. Tomlinson have classified the "architecture" of trees and treelike plants into twenty-six "models," based on the way the shoot system develops.[1] Their system was originated to classify the wide variety of tropical trees, but it applies to the more familiar and limited types of architecture of temperate trees. These differences in architecture are due primarily to differences in rates and patterns of growth, as discussed in chapter 1. The first six of their models are, however, plants like palms and tree ferns which have huge leaves and usually unbranched stems, or like banana plants which may reach the height of small trees by having gigantic leaves growing upward from a very short stem near ground level.

Whatever the architecture of a tree, the basic design creates problems that are not faced by prostrate plants and are not serious for small upright plants or for short-lived ones. The design of trees creates some special problems due to their size and complexity and to the limitations of the construction components, methods, and materials. This chapter will focus on some of the problems and the solutions trees have developed.

The first problem that plants faced as they evolved into upright forms, which is still the first problem a tree faces as it grows from a seed, is gravity. Gravity creates the constant downward pull that produces weight. Because of gravity, which is aided and abetted by wind, rain, and snow, the aerial parts of trees always tend to bend down. If they bend too much they break off. Land plants evolved from living in water where they were supported, to living prostrate on the ground, and then to living as erect, upright plants. The first solution to the gravity problem was for many plant parts to grow and orient themselves with respect to gravity. This oriented growth is called *geotropism*. Geotropism in trees is most obvious, and most studied, when the new shoot from a seed grows up and the new root grows down. Successive generations of branches or roots may not have as simple orientations, i.e., they may grow at some angle to vertical or they may have no geotropic response. Certainly, as a generalization, branches in the shoot system have a geotropic response that tends to keep them growing up. To achieve the objective of becoming the tallest plants, the uppermost shoots of a tree must grow up. The generalization that roots grow down is not nearly as valid. In a tree root system with millions of roots, relatively few actually grow down.

When shoots grow up very far, they soon have to develop sufficient strength to keep from being broken by their own weight or by the stresses produced from blowing in the wind. The solution was to develop wood, a tissue that specialized for strength by having its cells develop thick walls. The walls of wood cells of the first erect plants were made primarily of cellulose. Cellulose is a long-chain, regular molecule. Cotton fiber is an example of nearly pure cellulose. E. S. Barghoorn has suggested that cellulose walls were not really strong enough for tall plants and that an important evolutionary development was that land plants began to add lignin to cell walls for stiffening.[2] Lignin is a complex, highly branched molecule that in wood is essentially plastered on an oriented framework of cellulose. Lignin gives wood (and paper bags made from untreated wood pulp) its brown color. Lignin must be removed from wood pulp to make high-quality white paper. Nowadays just about all upright plants have cell walls with both cellulose and lignin. Wood of trees is usually about two-thirds cellulose or related carbohydrates and one-third lignin.

Wood cell walls are strong, but as a tree grows taller and bigger each year, the stresses at the base of the stem become so great that the tree will break. The problem cannot be solved by simply strengthening cell walls even further, because stronger materials than cellulose and lignin are not available. The only other solution is to make more cells, so as to make the stem and branches stronger by making them thicker. Many plants developed a special meristem, the cambium, which produced new wood cells. This is the solution used by trees where cambial activity is a major process in tree growth. Some treelike plants such as bamboo and tree ferns do not have cambium. Their stems are just as big around when the plant is short as when it is tall. There is no mechanism for thickening the stem once it is formed. This solution works, bamboo and tree ferns are common in parts of the world, but, because stem thickness cannot change, the stem cannot respond to different environmental demands. There is also a high cost in making a large stem when the plant is small and does not need it.

Another problem that arises as a tree gets tall is that it must be anchored securely in the ground. The solution of trees is to thicken the roots near the base of the stem by adding wood to make them stronger. Tree roots thicken just as the shoots do, but palms do not have a cambium in the roots and they solve the problem of anchoring by making more, relatively weak, roots near the base of the stem, rather than having the ones already present get thicker.

As the tree grows taller it needs more and more photosynthate for energy and building materials. To have more photosynthesis in trees that have relatively small leaves, the tree has to produce more leaves, the leaves cannot simply grow bigger. The solution is to branch and produce more leaf-bearing axes. This solution produces a large, exponential increase in leaf number. If a stem produces two branches each year and each branch produces two new branches each year, after four years there will be eighty new branches (fig. 3). If each one bears the same number of leaves,

| Year 1 | Year 2 | Year 3 | Year 4 |
| 2 branches | 8 branches | 26 branches | 80 branches |

3   TREE BRANCHING
Diagram of branching in a model tree where each shoot produces two
lateral branches each year.

then leaf number will have increased eighty times in four years.

As more leaves are produced they inevitably tend to shade
each other and reduce the amount of total photosynthesis. The
solution to the problem of mutual shading is to develop a branching pattern and leaf arrangement that minimizes overlapping. In
many trees the leaves are shaped and distributed almost like the
pieces in a jigsaw puzzle to form a leaf mosaic. H. Horn has
pointed out that leaves of some trees are arranged in a monolayer
around the outside of the crown, while other trees have leaves
distributed throughout the crown in a multilayer. The monolayer
seems to be best adapted to trees that grow in low light, in the
shade of other trees, while multilayers are more common in trees
that pioneer open areas where there is high light.[3]

As the crown of a tree grows, branches become shaded on the
lower and inner parts of the crown. As they are progressively
shaded they produce less and less photosynthate. The fate of
these branches demonstrates a general principle of efficiency that
is evident in many aspects of tree design. Branches are not maintained if they cost more in photosynthate for maintenance and
growth than they produce from new photosynthesis. Branches

once established seem to have to be self-sufficient for photosynthate. If one is unproductive, usually because its leaves are shaded, it is not supported by the others, but its growth slows and it ultimately dies. As a result, leaves tend to be concentrated at the edge of the crown unless the branching is sparse and the tree is growing in full sunlight so that light can penetrate to the interior of the crown.

Increasing the number of leaves causes a set of problems associated with maintaining a balanced system of leaves, shoots, stem, and roots. One major problem is that there is an inevitable water loss from leaves because water vapor diffuses out the special holes in the leaf surface (the *stomata*) as the carbon dioxide diffuses in for photosynthesis. The solution to the increased water loss is to increase the number of roots that are taking up water. There are feedback controls between the amount of leaves and the amount of roots so that they stay in balance. For instance, if there are too many leaves and not enough roots, water stress will increase in the leaves, leaf growth will stop, and root growth will continue until the system is in balance.[4]

As the tree gets bigger, more material must be transported from leaves to roots. All this transport is through cells and the rate is limited by physical restrictions. The solution is continually to make additional specialized transport cells. The cambium produces more cells, some of which differentiate into cells that transport water in the wood and others that transport photosynthate in the phloem, or inner bark.

The wood, therefore, has functions of both support and water transport. There seems to be an evolutionary sequence from primitive wood where one type of cell (tracheids) serves both transport and support functions to more advanced types of wood where some cells are specialized for water transport (vessels) and other cells are specialized for support (fibers).[5] In this evolutionary progression the vessels of more advanced wood become more specialized for water transport until they are basically long hollow tubes in the wood, tubes that are so wide that they can be seen by eye.

A problem associated with the longevity of trees is the high probability that parts of the tree will be injured. Various animals eat roots and twigs. Wind, snow, frost heaving, and so on can break off roots and branches. Such a loss is particularly important if the injured shoot is the main stem, because without replacement there can be no central, vertical shoot to serve the function of making the tree tall. The solution is to produce replacement shoots, or roots if the damage affects the root system, that grow in the same direction as the missing part and replace its function. There are three general responses to injury that generate replacement axes. One is to grow out tiny roots or shoots that have been stored in case of an injury. Another response is to create new roots or shoots after the injury. A third response is for existing axes to change orientation and take over the function of the injured axis. This last solution required the development of wood cells that could act to bend the preexisting branch upward. The first response has an advantage in that the lag time between injury and development of new axes is very short because the replacement axes were already present. The second response has an advantage because the number and position of new axes is not predetermined and can be sensitive to requirements resulting from a particular injury. The third response has the advantage of using an already existing, grown shoot as a replacement by changing its orientation, so the length of time to effect a replacement is determined solely by the length of time it takes for the reorientation.

Trees face some problems that they have not been able to solve over the hundreds of millions of years of their evolution. They seem to have an absolute maximum height of about 120 meters (about 400 feet). The tallest living trees are redwoods in California, about 110 meters tall, and eucalypts in Australia, over 100 meters tall. There are stories of taller trees that have since been cut, but they probably were less than 120 meters tall. These tallest trees grow in very favorable environments, with sun for photosynthesis, plenty of water, and a low frequency of storms over their life span of hundreds to thousands of years. There seem to be two major factors that eventually limit height growth of these huge trees. One is that the water stress inside a tree increases with height in the tree.[6] There are limitations that do not permit cells to grow if the water stress is too high, and the limiting water stress occurs at not much higher than 120 meters in trees. Trees have not evolved super cells that can grow at extremely high water stress. The other factor is that as trees get very tall they also must thicken at the bottom to keep from breaking off. They become so large that their own weight can cause structural problems.

Although trees have not solved the problem of growing infinitely tall, some species do seem to be able to live almost indefinitely, except, perhaps, for being able to survive long-term climatic changes. Individuals of other tree species may have relatively short life spans. There are two things that aid plants in becoming very old. Trees are particularly good at having extremely old stems. Many of the large conifers growing in the dense forests of the Pacific Northwest survive several thousand years. The record for stem old age, however, is held by bristlecone pines that survive under harsh conditions at high elevations in the mountains of the arid Southwest. These trees may grow for almost 5,000 years. Bristlecone pines are small trees that grow without competition from other plants, even from other bristlecone pines. The crowns of the trees are ragged and weather-beaten, but new vigorous shoots keep developing. Only thin strips of bark may still be alive, and dead parts of stems can even be eroded away by blowing sand, but parts of the stem stay alive. Bristlecone pines are certainly a contrast to the giant trees of the Northwest, but they seem to be able to grow indefinitely. Another technique that an individual plant has to enable it to survive over indefinite lengths of time is the ability to produce new shoots and stems as the old ones die, rot, and disappear. This method of survival is used by many plant forms, from grasses to trees.[7] Many trees produce shoot "sprouts" at the base of old stems if the old stem dies or is cut. Eventually the new stems form a ring around the rotten remains of the parent stump. Trees like poplars can produce shoot "suckers" from roots. Over long periods of time these new shoots may develop their own root systems and form a clone of separate stems that were originally all part of the same plant. This process can be repeated over and over as the old shoot dies and new ones develop. The plant may slowly spread over the landscape, moving from one place to another as it advances at the growing front and the oldest tissue dies to the rear. A tree like this has the capacity to survive indefinitely as a genetically continuous clone, even though no single stem survives very long.

Some plants have taken alternative routes to becoming tall. One major form that is successful is the vine, or liane. Vines use other plants as support and grow above them by literally growing on top of them. Without much need for strength, at least compared to what a free-standing tree requires, vines can put photosynthate otherwise required for wood production into shoot, root, and leaf production. The strangler fig uses a particularly sneaky strategy for becoming the tallest plant. The fig seeds are carried by birds and germinate high up on the bark of a host tree. The fig develops a relatively short stem-and-shoot system, but the roots grow all the way down to the ground on the surface of the tree bark. When the roots reach the ground and proliferate in the soil, the portions of the roots on the bark thicken and eventually coalesce to form a solid cylinder of woody root tissue on the outside of the stem of the host tree. The host tree eventually dies and the strangler fig "tree" is left as a tuft of shoot system on top of a fake stem built from woody roots.

A problem associated with sexual reproduction and seed production is that photosynthetic resources must be used to build all the new structures associated with seeds and fruits. Photosynthate used in reproduction cannot be used for the growth of the shoot or root system. Years of heavy seed and fruit production are often marked by the reduced growth of the rest of the tree. After flowering, annual species allocate almost all their photosynthate to seeds and fruits and when sexual reproduction is finished the vegetative structure of the plant dies. Given the general objective of trees to grow into tall, long-lived structures, a tree cannot afford periods of reduced growth if they affect its ability to compete with other trees. Trees solve this problem in several ways. They delay sexual reproduction for years or decades. During this "juvenile" period the tree is not capable of flowering. All the photosynthate goes into growth and maintenance to establish rapidly the structure of the tree. Forest geneticists have had success in artificially shortening the juvenile period by applying growth regulators, especially high concentrations of gibberellins. When the tree eventually does mature it can flower, but it may not flower every year. Many trees have years of heavy seed bearing separated by periods of several years of light seed bearing. Shaded trees usually flower little, if at all. Generally, trees become mature earlier and flower earlier and more abundantly where there is adequate light and little competition. Thus, trees seem to defer flowering until they have grown into a dominant position with adequate light where photosynthate is abundant and where a decrease in growth will not affect survival.

THE INDIVIDUAL ROOT and shoot axes grow by additive processes. New cells are added to make them thicker or longer so the total size is the sum of all the additions. The growth in total number of axes each year is multiplicative because the rate is determined by the number of parent axes multiplied by the branching rate per axis. Later in the book we will look at how tree axes are connected together in a structure with regular patterns; this chapter will describe how additive and multiplicative growth of the population of root and shoot axes occurs in the tree.

Both additive and multiplicative growth in trees is from meristems. Meristems are localized areas of axes that act as cell-producing factories. They cause elongation, thickening, and branching. Meristems produce new cells by division, the cells then enlarge and subsequently differentiate into one of the many cell types that make up a tree. Apical meristems at the tip of each growing root and shoot produce cells for elongation of axes, and they also produce the cells that form new meristems. There are lateral meristems—the cambium between the wood and bark and the cork cambium within the bark—that produce cells for the thickening of axes and also produce more meristem cells to increase the size of the lateral meristem, which is a parallel to branching in apical meristems.

Elongation and thickening occur through the production of files of cells—longitudinal files in apical meristems and radial files in cambia (fig. 4). As the files get longer through the addition of new cells by the meristem, the axis elongates or thickens. The increase in length of files of cells to produce elongation and thickening is a result of both cell division to produce new cells in a file and the subsequent enlargement of each new cell. Although cell

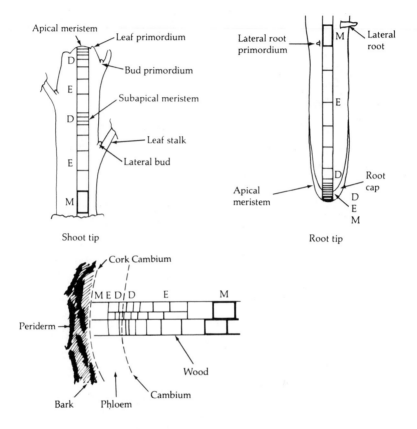

4   FILES FROM MERISTEMS

Diagrams of sample radial files produced by meristems. Each file has zones of cell division (D), enlargement (E), and maturation or wall differentiation (M). Shoot and root apical meristems form lateral buds or roots. The cambium forms new files of cells. The cork cambium forms new periderm layers in the bark.

size may vary throughout a year in a file of cells, there is surprisingly little difference between cell size in a fast- or slow-
growing file. The major differences in the amount of elongation
or thickening are due to the number of cells in a file. The number
of cells is determined by the number of cell divisions that create
the new cells. Therefore, differences in amounts of growth are
due primarily to differences in the numbers of cell divisions in
meristems.

Because of the additive nature of tree growth the youngest cells
in a file are in the meristems where cell divisions occur. Therefore, distance from a meristem is related to the time since a cell, or
tissue, was formed. The youngest leaves are nearest the apical
meristem that formed them and the oldest the furthest away.
Wood is youngest at the outside of the tree near the cambial meristem and oldest on the inside. A sequence of cells, tissues, or
organs at increasing distances from the meristem that formed
them also represents a developmental sequence in time. Scientists studying development in trees, or in any plants that grow
from meristems, often use the technique of substituting space for
time. For example, it is easier to study a sequence of branches
from the top to the bottom of a tree, each branch a year older, than
to wait while a particular branch grows over the years. Because
a record of cambial activity is stored in the wood and a record of
annual elongation in the shoot and root systems, it is also possible to work backward through space and time to see how a particular shoot or root has developed over the years. One problem
with this technique is that it is not possible to reconstruct the
whole history of a tree because many shoots and roots, and of
course the leaves, have died and disappeared over the years.

Meristems also produce new meristems. The shoot apical meristem produces lateral leaves that grow by short-lived meristems.
The shoot or root apical meristems also produce lateral shoot
or root meristems that grow into lateral branches each with its
own apical meristem. New cambial meristem, to accommodate

the increasing girth of the cambium as an axis thickens, is produced from existing cambial meristem by special cell divisions. New cambial meristem is also formed in axes created by shoot and root elongation. It arises from undifferentiated cells produced by the apical meristems. Later the cambial meristem expands circumferentially by producing new meristem cells of its own.

Division and cell enlargement are localized near the meristem. Therefore growth only occurs immediately adjacent to meristems. The tissue that has been formed in the past is stored as the bulk of the tree, except for leaves and other parts that die and are lost. Most of the tree, once formed, stays the same. A wire fence nailed to a tree is an example of the stability of nonmeristematic parts of trees. As the years pass, the fence stays at the same height on the tree, because elongation occurs only near apical meristems at the tip of the tree and at the end of each branch. As the tree grows in diameter, wood grows over the nail and the wire. The wire does not move and new wood is added outside the old wood. Therefore, the wire is buried in the tree marking the height and year it was first put up. Once buried, cambial activity and radial enlargement occur on the outside of the tree, beyond the wire.

This localization of current growth and storing up of previous growth permits some detective work to measure growth from previous years. It is easiest to measure previous growth in temperate trees that have annual seasons of growth and nongrowth. In many of these trees the annual elongation of each shoot is marked by successive groups of bud-scale scars on the surface of the bark and the annual thickening of the wood is marked by annual rings (fig. 5). Detective work on previous growth is not always easy. Not all trees have bud-scale scars and some produce more than one set of bud-scale scars per year, but in these cases there may be other clues to the amount of elongation. For instance, the pattern of branching often is annual. Many trees

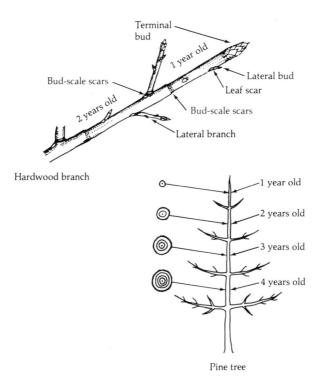

Hardwood branch

Pine tree

5 ANNUAL DIVISIONS OF SHOOTS

Divisions are marked on the outside of shoots by bud-scale scars or groups of long branches and in the wood by the number of annual rings.

growing in the tropics produce no rings in the wood at all. Some trees may produce more than one ring each year, either because of injury or because of distinct flushes of growth. In general, it is difficult to work out previous growth rates in the root system. There are no bud scales, there is usually no annual pattern of branching, and growth rings in the wood are difficult to see and frequently do not go all the way around the root.

The files of cells that meristems produce arise because cells divide and redivide in the same plane, perpendicular to the axis of the file (see fig. 4). As cells from a meristem are added to the file, they pass through phases of division, enlargement, and differentiation. Because adjacent cells tend to be in the same phase of development, there are zones of division, enlargement, and differentiation in the files. This process of cell production and file development is easiest to visualize in cambial activity. The general processes are similar in longitudinal files from apical meristems, but there may be major differences between files from the center to the outside of the root or shoot axes. In shoot apical meristems a few cells in each file may begin to divide again after the rest have stopped. These bands, or slices, of dividing cells form subapical meristems that are important in producing new cells in files. Both root apical meristems and cambial meristems actually produce radial files in two directions. In roots, the root cap is produced outward and the bulk of the root, inward. In the cambium, the wood is produced to the inside and phloem to the outside, while the cork cambium produces cork to the outside and thin-walled cells to the inside.

New leaves and buds are produced from localized divisions in surface layers of the shoot apical meristems, essentially areas where meristematic activity continues, as is shown in figure 4. These new meristems are called *primordia* when they are very small. Tiny protrusions from the surface of the meristem, the leaf primordia, form first. They are produced in regular sequences, either in spirals in alternate-leaved plants, or in successive opposite pairs in opposite-leaved plants. These primordia eventually develop into leaves through the activity of short-lived terminal and marginal meristems found only in leaves. Soon after the leaves begin to develop, bud primordia form associated with each leaf, usually on the stem just above the leaf base. The bud primordia soon differentiate to form new shoot apical meristems that can form new lateral shoots when branching occurs.

New lateral root primordia form inside roots in a tissue that has remained undifferentiated (see fig. 4). These primordia form ᵥᵧ ᵥᵥᵥlized divisions to develop a small cluster of meristematic cells. The root primordium soon differentiates into a root apical meristem, which later grows out through the side of the root. Lateral root primordia are not formed in regular sequences as are leaf and bud primordia, but they usually develop in several lines along the root.

The cambium does not produce lateral appendages, but it does enlarge as the tree grows by adding new meristem that forms new files. As apical meristems elongate, the cambium is extended into the new axes by cells in an inner cylinder of tissue that have already elongated but that begin to redivide to form new cambium and new radial files of wood and phloem cells. This formation of new meristem by redivision of cells from the apical meristems is somewhat comparable to the formation of lateral leaf, shoot, and root primordia by redivision of cells in special areas, except that in the cambium the new meristem forms a complete cylinder rather than discrete clusters of cells as it does in the primordia.

There are two basic cell types in the cambium. Fusiform cells are long, needle-shaped cells oriented longitudinally. Ray cells are rectangular, relatively short, and radially oriented. Each cell type produces files of cells of its own type. Fusiform cells ultimately constitute 70 to 90 percent of the wood and function primarily in water transport and mechanical support. Ray cells make up the rest of the wood and function primarily in transporting materials from the outside to the inside of the tree. Ray cells are usually aggregated into units called *rays*. Rays are large enough to see in many hardwoods, particularly in oak. They appear as lines or stripes across the annual rings.

New cambial meristem is also formed by occasional special cell divisions within existing cambium (fig. 6). Most divisions are oriented so that the new walls are perpendicular to the axis of the radial files. These divisions increase cell numbers in the files. Sometimes, however, a division will occur so that the new wall is

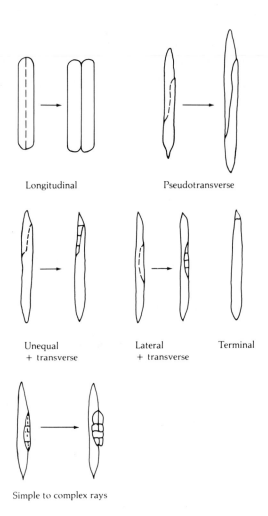

Longitudinal

Pseudotransverse

Unequal
+ transverse

Lateral
+ transverse

Terminal

Simple to complex rays

6 CAMBIAL DIVISIONS

Types of divisions producing new fusiform and ray cambial cells.

parallel to the radial axis and a new meristematic cell is produced. This new meristematic cell can then produce a new radial file. This mechanism increases the number of both fusiform and ray files as the cambium increases in girth.

There are a number of types of divisions that produce new cambial cells from parent fusiform cambial cells. The parent cell may be divided by a straight wall from end-to-end of the cell to produce two daughter cells the same length as the parent. The new dividing wall is, however, frequently not straight. It may be S-shaped and not run the length of the cell (a pseudotransverse division);[1] it may cut out one side of the cell (a lateral division); it may just cut off the tip of the cell. Divisions that produce daughter cells of about equal size usually produce new fusiform cells. Where divisions produce daughter cells markedly unequal in size the smaller cell either becomes directly a ray cell or becomes, through subsequent redivisions, a series of ray cells.[2] Thus, fusiform parent cells can produce either new fusiform or new ray cells in the cambium.

Cork cambium produces most of the hard part of the bark in trees. It produces cork to the outside of the tree and, in most cases, just a few cells to the inside. The general operation of a cork cambium is similar to the cambium, but there are no ray cells. Cork cells are in radial files produced by oriented divisions in the meristem, just like wood cells. There is a tremendous variation in the extent and longevity of cork cambia in different tree species. Trees with thin, smooth bark, like beech, have a long-lived cork cambium that forms a sheath around the tree stem just as the cambium does and expands as the stem thickens. Trees with rough bark, however, have many cork cambia, each of small area and relatively short-lived. New cork cambia keep forming under the old ones in these trees.

Cork cambia form in a process analogous to the formation of cambium in new root and shoot axes. The first cambia form in tissue produced by the apical meristem. Adjacent cells just under the outer surface of the stem begin to divide to produce a sheet of meristem that then forms radial files. In trees where the cork cambia are short-lived, successive cambia are formed by similar processes of localized sheets of division underneath the old cork cambia. After a while new cork cambia begin to form in old phloem tissue produced by the cambium. As these successive cambia form underneath each other and the tree expands in girth the bark develops ridges or plates of dead corky tissue to the outside. Bark may peel, or separate and fall off, through layers of weak, thin-walled cells in the cork or between successive cork cambia. Some birches have bark that peels off in strips. In some trees, like sycamore or, most spectacularly, in some eucalypt species, the older layers of bark fall off the tree, leaving the younger, lighter-colored layers exposed. I have seen eucalypt trees where the dark gray outer bark is shed to reveal a creamy white layer of bark, which gradually turns pink and then gray. The change of bark colors is as dramatic as the autumn coloring in leaves of deciduous trees.

The growth and proliferation of root and shoot axes in a tree is entirely from meristematic activity. Meristems are tiny, but they are absolutely vital to trees. As a result they are protected, by leaves or bud scales, the root cap, or the bark. There are also mechanisms by which new meristems can be regenerated in undifferentiated tissue if the old meristems are destroyed. Meristems may be easy to overlook in a tree, but their importance cannot be overemphasized.

BRANCHES IN THE shoot or root system develop in patterns with different levels of organization. The simplest level is determined by the nature of lateral formation in apical meristems. Branches grow from the sides of a parent axis. Therefore, it is convenient to classify branches by order, with orders being comparable to generations in populations. The main axis is called the first order, all branches off the first order are called the second order, all branches off the second order are called the third order, and so on (fig. 7).

Branches are not formed randomly. In the shoot system they are in successive pairs (opposite), or in a spiral (alternate), in a regular pattern called *phyllotaxy* that is determined in the apical meristem. In the root system, laterals are usually in rows along the parent root, with successive laterals somewhat evenly spaced, but not as completely regular as they are in the shoot system.

Another level of complexity is that each higher order usually elongates more slowly than the parent order. Root systems have a relatively simple basic pattern resulting from the fairly regular spacing of laterals and the slower growth of each higher order (fig. 8). The pattern becomes more complex because successive branches may not elongate at the same rate. Many shoot systems have annually repeating patterns where the uppermost, youngest lateral branches on each annual shoot increment are the longest, with a decrease in length of laterals down to the lowermost, oldest lateral of that year, which is the shortest (fig. 9).

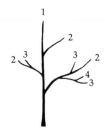

Shoot order numbers

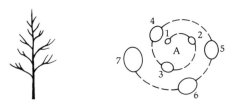

Alternate (spiral) phyllotaxy

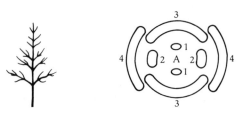

Opposite phyllotaxy

7   BRANCH AND LEAF RELATIONSHIPS

Branches are related to each other by order number. The position of origin of both branches and leaves is determined by phyllotaxy. Diagrams of phyllotaxy show branch positions on the left and the apical meristems (A) on the right with the sequence of leaves. Leaf 1 is the youngest.

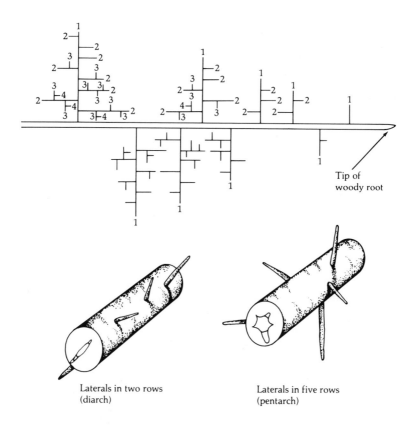

Laterals in two rows
(diarch)

Laterals in five rows
(pentarch)

8   ROOT BRANCHING PATTERNS

The long woody root above bears four orders of fine roots. Lateral fine roots may be in two to five or more rows.

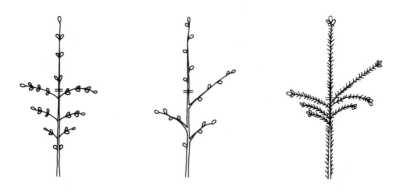

9. SHOOT BRANCHING PATTERNS
Typical patterns in temperate trees with opposite branching (left), alternate branching (center), and apparent whorled branching from a tight spiral in pine (right).

This pattern is particularly marked in trees like pines where the main branches develop in such tight spirals that they appear to be in whorls and the lower laterals are reduced to minute short shoots bearing the needles. Such patterns of differentiation between successive branches may be annual, or they may be repeated several times during a year in trees that have more than one flush of growth. At even another level of pattern in shoot systems there may be differential growth between laterals growing from the upper or lower side of a parent shoot (fig. 10).

The initial pattern of branching is simplified in older branches where many small branches have died and been lost and there has been differential thickening of the remaining branches. In older trees, the basal portion of the stem is the thickest part of the tree and is essentially free of branches, but the terminal portions of the root and shoot systems are still growing with the same basic pattern. F. Hallé, R. A. A. Oldeman, and P. B. Tomlinson showed that new vigorous shoots that develop in old shoot systems of tropical trees show the basic pattern of the species that may have been lost in the older tree.[1] They call this process *reiteration*.

The form of a shoot or root system is essentially what it looks like from a distance, or what an artist might draw to represent a tree if most of the detail had to be omitted. It is the sum of many years' accumulation of patterns, simplified by the death of some older branches and the accentuation by thickening of others. Describing the form of a root system is somewhat absurd, because a root system cannot be seen at a distance, indeed it cannot be seen at all because it is in the soil. However, parts of root systems can be seen after the soil has been washed out or excavated, and the rest can be visualized. Few of the small branches can be seen at a distance or, in the case of root systems, they have been removed, so most of the form of a shoot or root system results from the older, thicker framework that bears the leaves or smaller roots.

Form and pattern in tree growth is remarkably consistent. Over the life of a tree many apical meristems are injured by pests or the elements and yet the pattern and form is maintained. Both shoot and root systems have developed mechanisms whereby injured axes are replaced by laterals that bend to grow in the same direction as their parent axis and functionally replace the parent in the branching pattern.

THE SHOOT SYSTEM

Young trees generally have a pyramidal form with a single central stem and a crown that is broad at the base and tapered to a pointed top. Most conifer species (pines, spruces, firs, etc.) re-

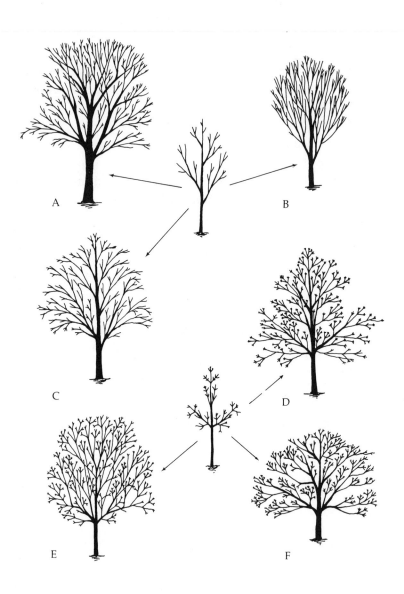

tain this pyramidal form as they grow older. Only a few deciduous angiosperm trees (hardwoods) (e.g., pin oak) keep a pyramidal form. The pyramidal form results from a pattern of branch growth where the central stem is dominant, the second-order branches grow out at a wide angle, and, going down from the top, second-order branches are longer because they are older.

In most hardwood trees the pyramidal form begins to change as the tree grows. The central stem is lost in the top of the tree, as a number of equally dominant, nearly vertical, branches develop, and the top of the tree becomes rounded. This forking of the main stem usually occurs nearer the ground in those trees grown in the open than in those grown in the forest. In some oaks the transition to multiple stems occurs as lateral branches near the top begin to elongate and thicken as much as, or more than, the main stem. In other species the main stem is injured or does not develop, and a fork is produced from replacement, lateral shoots. Meanwhile, the lowest branches begin to grow more slowly because they are shaded, so the bottom of the crown also becomes

10   WARD'S SILHOUETTES
Silhouette models reproduced from H. M. Ward, *Trees*, vol. 5: *Form and Habit* (Cambridge University Press, 1909). Starting with alternate (above) or opposite (below) branching in young pyramidal trees, different patterns of branch development result in different forms. Above: if a few laterals develop and outward buds are favored, it is like some lindens (A); if laterals develop equally and new laterals develop at the tip of the parent axes, it is like willow and poplar (B); if there is outward curvature and almost pendant branches, it is like a wych elm (C). Below: if more vigorous growth of *inwardly* directed buds and if the tips stop so that the laterals grow out forming dichotomies, you get lilac (D); if more vigorous growth of *outwardly* directed buds you get maple (E); if downward and outward growth with recurved tips it is like horse-chestnut in the open (F).

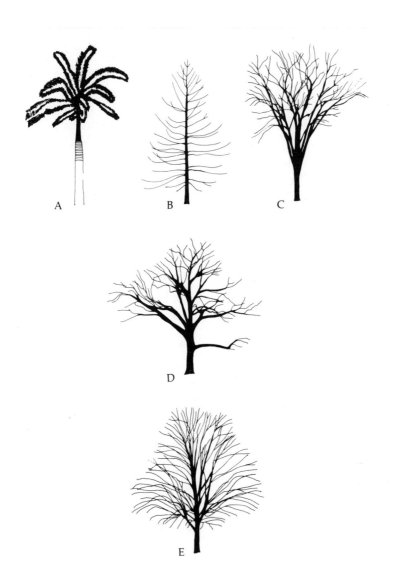

11   SILHOUETTES
(A) palm, (B) larch, (C) elm, (D) oak, (E) maple, (F) weeping beech, (G) fastigiate linden.

G

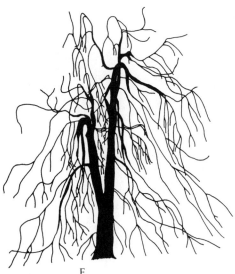

F

rounded. The result is an oval crown with a central stem at the base. This is the typical shape of maples planted as shade trees. Unfortunately for most homeowners, it may take some time for a newly planted tree to develop the typical mature form of the species. Old trees usually develop flattened tops as the branches all reach the same general height. As the tree becomes very old branches begin to die in the top of the crown.

There are many types of form (fig. 11). The stem may be subdivided into a number of equal branches, all of which turn upward at the base, but outward at the tip, to form a vase-shaped tree like amur cork tree. In American elm the main stem forks when the tree is quite young. Each part of the fork grows upward and bends out. This process of forking followed by upward growth that bends out continues as the arching crown of the mature tree develops. This arching crown was a common sight along streets of cities and towns throughout America before Dutch elm disease destroyed most of these beautiful shade trees.

There are some fascinating variations of form which are propagated for horticultural purposes. Fastigiate forms, like the linden or Lombardy poplar, have branches that grow up almost vertically and a crown that is very narrow. Weeping forms like the common weeping willow or the dramatic weeping beech and pines have branches that droop down to the ground. There are even prostrate forms of some tree species, which grow close to the ground, developing mounds of branches with no semblance of a central stem. Dwarf forms are popular for some types of plantings or for indoors. They may be genetic dwarfs where growth rates are drastically reduced, or they may be dwarfed by pruning and special growth conditions, like the tiny bonsai trees that are only a few feet tall but that may be several hundreds of years old. One of the most unusual forms is a European beech with branches that grow out like a cork screw.

Trees of the same species grown in different environments usually have different forms. In general, trees growing in the open have full, symmetrical crowns with leaves relatively near the ground, but in forest-grown trees the lower branches are shaded and die so that only the upper part of the crown survives. Trees growing along a roadside in a forest often have well-developed crowns toward the road where there is light (unless that side is damaged by pollution from the road), and very little crown away from the road where development is suppressed by shading from other trees. Trees growing in harsh environments, for instance arid areas, are usually shorter and more compact because the branches are closer together. Trees grown high on mountains or near the seashore may be both shortened and shaped by the wind. There may be almost no branches on the side toward the wind and relatively good branch development on the side away from the wind.

BRANCHING PATTERN AND LEAF DISPLAY

The branching patterns in trees seem to be designed to display leaves effectively. The major objective in leaf display is to get the most net photosynthate production that can be used to build the tree. Net photosynthate is the amount of photosynthate produced by leaves minus the amount that it costs to build, display, and maintain the leaves. The problem is that leaves produce less photosynthate in the shade as light intensity decreases. Therefore, there can be only a limited number of layers of leaves before the bottom layer is so deeply shaded by those above it that the lowest leaves cannot produce enough photosynthate to survive. Following the general principle of efficiency, branches with leaves that do not produce any net photosynthate will die because they will not be supported by photosynthate from the rest of the tree.

A secondary objective, but a vitally important one in arid countries, is to keep leaf temperature and transpirational water loss as low as possible. Trees growing under dry conditions have leaves arranged to reduce light absorption in the middle of the day—for instance, they may have leaves that hang down or that have highly reflective surfaces—and to increase the efficiency of cooling by having small leaves in an open crown.[2]

New leaves form only at the ends of branches where they are made by apical meristems. In trees that lose their leaves every year, the only leaves are at the ends of branches. Leaves in the interior of the crown must be produced by persistent short shoots. Evergreen trees keep their leaves for more than one year. There are many evergreen species, for instance, some oaks, tropical broad-leaved trees, eucalypts, and, of course, conifers like pines. Leaves may only live a few years, but the record of fifty years is held by the bristlecone pine.[3] Leaves seem to last longer on evergreen trees that are growing slowly, either because they are in the shade or because they are in arid conditions, which is the case with the bristlecone pine. Within the crown of most red pines, leaves last only two years on well-lit branches, but they may last four or more years on lower, shaded branches.

One solution to the problem of displaying leaves to get more light is to make branches that grow out horizontally so the leaf-bearing tips are not shaded by branches above. Unfortunately, there are high costs involved in building long branches, particularly horizontal branches that must be very strong to avoid sagging or breaking. In open-grown trees this solution works for a while, and at least the leaves at the end of the branches are in the sun. In forest-grown trees a horizontal branch soon grows under the crown of a neighboring tree and is shaded. Even in open-grown trees there is a limit to the length of horizontal branches. At some point it costs more photosynthate to display leaves at the end of long horizontal branches than the leaves can produce. Many trees such as oaks have very long branches, but they do not extend indefinitely. Some fig trees have solved the problem of branch length by developing roots from the underside of their lower branches. These roots grow down to the ground, branch in the soil, and then thicken from cambial activity. After a while the roots are strong enough to support the branch. The branch can continue to grow out, supported by its roots, almost indefinitely. The central stem can even die and rot away because the branch now has its own root system.

Given that branches are constrained by having a maximum length, the branching pattern can help display leaves for efficient light absorption. In vertical branches and in trees growing in high light intensity, the leaves are distributed in a multilayer so that light penetrates into the canopy; but if they are growing in the shade, leaves are distributed in horizontal monolayers to reduce mutual shading.[4] These horizontal layers of leaves are called *leaf mosaics* because the leaves fit so closely together (fig. 12). The leaves themselves help form leaf mosaics by several mechanisms. The first leaves are usually the biggest and successive leaves are smaller. The combination of the spiral, or opposite, leaf arrangement and the different leaf sizes means that leaves on a vertical shoot have little overlap. In many cases leaves on vertical shoots that are in full sunlight are tilted down. This angle permits them to absorb enough light for maximum photosynthesis, but also reduces leaf temperature and allows light to pass through to leaves below. On horizontal shoots the leaves coming from the upper side are usually smaller than those from the lower side, and the petioles of the leaves twist so that all the leaf blades are in the same horizontal plane.

The leaves on each shoot are arranged in a mosaic, but in addition the shoots are arranged in a branching pattern that produces a larger mosaic. In a common pattern, lateral long shoots occur at intervals and are separated by a number of short shoots. With this pattern, leaves from the long shoots do not overlap those from the short shoots. When the long shoots elongate, higher-order branches develop that fill in the spaces. The long shoots explore into new areas and the short shoots fill in the new areas. Leaves

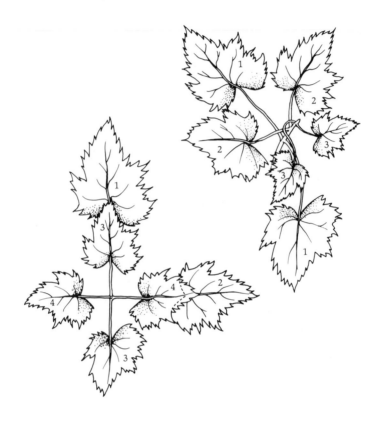

12   LEAF MOSAICS

Aerial view of leaf arrangements in a vertical maple shoot (left) and a horizontal maple shoot (right) showing differences in leaf blade and stalk size.

on shoots are only formed on current growth, so as the shoot grows each year the position of the new leaves changes. Short shoots, however, scarcely elongate, so the leaves stay essentially in the same position for a number of years.

There are some elaborate variations on this theme of long shoots and short shoots arranged to make a leaf mosaic, particularly in tropical trees.[5] It is tempting to think that these patterns are designed (have evolved) to optimize some aspect of leaf display. For one tropical species that has a large leaf mosaic consisting of many shoots, analysis has shown that the angles between the branches on the tree are almost exactly the angles that a computer model predicts would be most efficient for leaf display.[6]

Light does not come to leaves only from directly above. Light comes from the whole sky (skylight) and, within the crown, light is reflected in all directions so the underside of leaves is not totally dark. Crowns with widely separated groups of major second-order branches permit the skylight to penetrate into the crown. At high latitudes the sun is not overhead, but displaced toward the equator. Many conifers growing near the Arctic have very narrow, long crowns and the trees are isolated. This design permits the crowns to utilize the light coming in at an angle. It is also efficient in reducing the snow load.

A variation on branching pattern and leaf display is the compound leaf.[7] A compound leaf with its leaflets has the same effect as a branch bearing leaves because the leaflets fit together to form a mosaic. Compound leaves have an advantage over very large single leaves because the smaller leaflets cool faster. They also can grow out rapidly and they cost less photosynthate than do many small leaves because they do not need to be permanent. The twigs bearing compound leaves are usually larger than those bearing small, simple leaves because the leaves need a large transport system and the twigs must be strong to support such large leaves. Compound leaves have the disadvantage that they

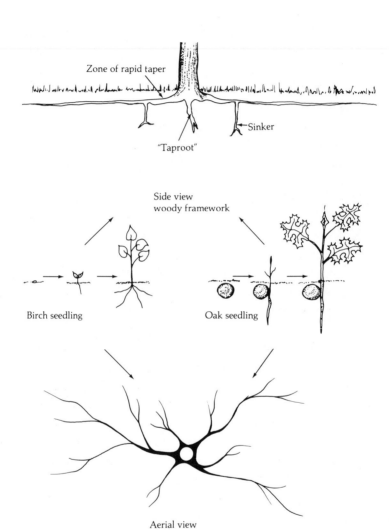

Zone of rapid taper

Sinker

"Taproot"

Side view
woody framework

Birch seedling

Oak seedling

Aerial view
woody framework

13   FORM OF ROOT SYSTEMS

are risky, for example, if one bud or one leaf is damaged, a large leaf area is lost.

THE ROOT SYSTEM

The form of a root system changes dramatically as the tree grows (fig. 13). The form of the initial root system of a tree seedling depends mostly on the size of the seed. Small seeds like birch produce a small root that grows downward. The small root cannot readily penetrate surface leaves and is easily deflected sideways. The root from a small seed cannot grow very long on stored food in the seed. Therefore, birch seedlings seldom survive on the fallen leaves and debris of the forest floor. When a small seed does germinate on a suitable seedbed, the small root soon branches into other small roots and there is never a distinct taproot. Large seeds produce large taproots that can penetrate leaves and grow down for a long way using the stored food. Acorns are large seeds that can germinate and survive on a wide variety of seedbeds because of the ability of their root to grow down to suitable conditions. Roots from large seeds usually form taproots reminiscent of carrots. These taproots have lateral roots that are very small. Intermediate-size seeds like those of a maple may or may not form taproots, depending on the difficulty of penetrating the surface layers of the soil.

Mature root systems are usually dominated by horizontal woody roots often twenty or more meters (sixty feet) long. Despite the fact that it is convenient to call them *horizontal* roots, it might be more accurate to say that they tend to grow at a consistent depth in the soil. They do not really grow horizontally, but tend to conform to the surface of the ground. Despite the myth that all trees have a large taproot, most trees have only remnants of it. The very few that actually do retain it are usually growing on deep sands. Trees often have a few woody roots, called *sinkers*, growing vertically down fairly near the stem, but otherwise most roots do not grow down. Measurements from all over the world show that in forests most of the roots are concentrated in the surface layers and that the number of roots decreases rapidly with increasing depth, so that most of the root tips are found within the uppermost fifteen centimeters (six inches) of the soil.

Comparable to the woody framework of the shoot system bearing leaves, the woody framework of the root system bears numerous fine roots. The root tips that form the woody roots of the framework are relatively large in diameter and elongate rapidly, up to a meter (three feet) in a year. The lateral roots from these large tips have small tips that form fine roots. The fine roots branch and rebranch to form many orders of roots. The fine roots are relatively short-lived, so the older portions of the woody framework are usually almost free of laterals. In fact, the death rate of fine roots is so high that a significant mass of roots dies each year.[8] As in the shoot system, the large root tips elongate rapidly into new areas, which the slow-growing fine roots exploit.

This separation into two types of tips, a relatively few large root tips (in the hundreds) and huge numbers of small root tips (Walter Lyford has estimated 90 million fine root tips in a mature red oak's root system),[9] is fairly common. However, not all root systems have clear-cut differences between roots with large tips and those with small tips. There may be intermediate-sized tips, but in all cases, by far the largest number of tips is the small tips.

Where do the large root tips come from? Many seedling root systems have no large diameter tips, and those with large diameter tap roots have lateral roots with small tips, yet mature root systems have many large diameter tips. The initial source of large root tips is the slow radial enlargement of lateral root apical meristems that takes place as the roots elongate. The small-diameter, fine root tips gradually enlarge over several years to

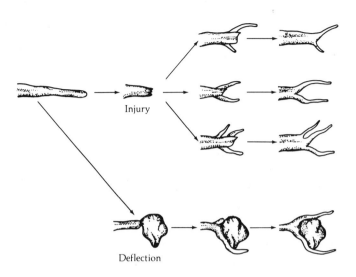

Injury

Deflection

14 FORKING IN WOODY ROOTS

Usually the large tips of woody roots form small lateral roots, but after injury or deflection they may form large laterals that grow to make forks in the woody framework.

become large-diameter tips. Once these large tips have formed their multiplication can occur in several ways. In systems with two distinct sizes of roots (e.g., red maple), large root tips normally produce only lateral roots with small tips. When a large tip is injured, however, it forms replacement lateral tips that are large in diameter. Usually several replacement tips are formed and the woody root forks where it was injured (fig. 14). Large lateral tips frequently develop when a large tip runs into a rock in the soil and is forced to grow very slowly as it bends around the rock. The large lateral usually develops so that it is going in the opposite direction from the parent tip. In some species, large lateral tips may also develop when the growth of the parent tip is slowed by low soil temperatures. The common factor seems to be that if the apical meristem is active, laterals with small tips develop, but if the apical meristem is inactive or destroyed, laterals with tips as large as the parent tip are then formed.

Vertical sinkers in the woody root system seem to originate from tip enlargement. For unknown reasons, a few laterals that formed when the tree was quite young, and that formed growing vertically downward, undergo tip enlargement even though adjacent tips develop into fine roots.

Roots do not have the problem of mutual shading and display that shoots do. Roots also do not have to support themselves, because they are supported by the soil. What the successful root system must do is to find suitable areas of the soil where water and minerals are plentiful and then multiply rapidly in these areas. Therefore, root systems are much more variable in form than shoot systems because they are growing in and adapting to a much more variable environment. Root systems seem to be organized developmentally to sample a large volume of soil and to proliferate in those portions where water and nutrients are relatively abundant while roots that grow into unsuitable areas die. For example, root systems are flat and shallow in swamps because the roots of most species cannot survive below the permanent water table where the water is oxygen deficient.

Just as the productivity of the shoot system depends on leaf area for light absorption, the uptake of water and nutrients is determined primarily by the surface area of the roots and particularly of the root tips. It is surprising that tree roots seldom have root hairs, but many tree roots are helped immensely in increasing surface area by forming mycorrhizae. Mycorrhizae are modified roots that develop when fungal hyphae (minute strands of the underground portion of fungi that form mushrooms or other underground fruiting bodies) grow into the root tip. The presence of the hyphae modifies the growth of the tip so that in many species mycorrhizal tips are morphologically distinct from non-mycorrhizal tips. The two organisms in mycorrhizae help each other. The root supplies carbohydrates to the fungus for use in fungal growth and the fungus, through its vast surface area in the soil, contributes nutrients to the root.[10] Mycorrhizae are particularly efficient in accumulating phosphorus from soils. Trees growing in nutrient-deficient soils grow much better if they can form mycorrhizae. Pines from America often grow poorly when planted in areas of Australia where the soils are mineral deficient and the mycorrhizal fungi are not present. In many cases this poor growth can be reversed by adding soil with the appropriate mycorrhizal fungus when planting the pines. At present many researchers are testing the effects of different mycorrhizal fungi on tree growth so that seedlings in nurseries can be infected with the most suitable fungus.

GROWTH IS DIRECTLY regulated where it occurs, at the meristems (fig. 15). Growth rates may be determined by the amount of various growth factors (the material actually used to build new cells), by growth regulators (hormones and inhibitors), or by the cell environment (temperature, physical stress on the cells, and water stress). Growth is regulated indirectly by the rates of uptake, synthesis, and transport which affect the level of growth factors or regulators at the actual site of growth. The basic materials for building trees are carbon dioxide, light energy, oxygen, nutrients, and water taken into the tree from the environment. These materials are used to synthesize the array of chemical compounds used in the plant. The growth factors and growth regulators are then transported to the meristems. Thus, any of the rates of uptake from the environment, or of synthesis or transport, may determine the level of growth factors at the meristem and, indirectly, the growth rate. The cell environment is closely related to the external environment. Temperature inside a meristem is determined primarily by the external air or soil temperature and by the amount of heating from light absorption. The physical stress levels within a meristem are determined by the pressures between the various cells, but the pressures may be modified by swaying in the wind or by injury. Water stress is determined by several factors—the rate of water uptake of the roots, the rate of loss through transpiration from the leaves, the increased stress with height in the tree, and the increased stress associated with water transport through the xylem.

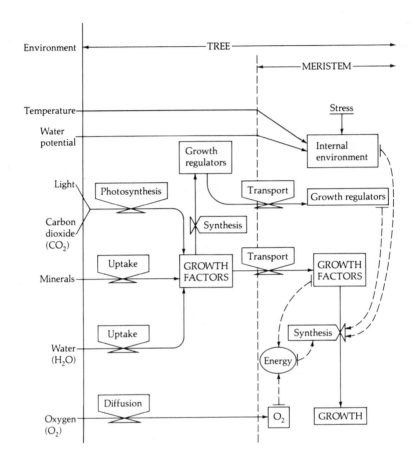

15   GROWTH REGULATION AT MERISTEMS

Relational diagram showing the interaction of external and internal growth regulation. Valve symbols are rates, boxes are levels, underlined values are constants not affected by the system as defined.

The regulation of growth is complex. This complexity permits cells with the same genetic information to develop into the tremendous array of cell types, tissue types, and organ types that grow in a tree. In addition to control by various rates, regulation also depends on the relative levels of growth factors and growth regulators and the stage of development of the cells that are growing. Different ratios of growth regulators may totally change the course of cell differentiation. The same ratio may cause different types of growth at different temperatures or if pressures between cells change. The same set of conditions will cause different growth in different type, size, or age meristems. Complex regulation permits close control of growth process. However, the regulation system is so complicated and varied that it is difficult to make valid generalizations. Scientists know in detail how some aspects of growth are controlled in some systems, but the regulation is often different in different systems.

The first step in making the substances that are growth factors at meristems is getting the raw materials from the external environment. The most important process, the point of everything else, is photosynthesis. Photosynthesis is a process that takes energy from the sunlight, carbon dioxide from the air, and water from the soil to make sugars. Carbon dioxide diffuses into the leaves through specialized groups of cells in the epidermis with valvelike openings called *stomata* (fig. 16). The rate of diffusion is regulated primarily by the size of the openings in the stomata. The stomata open in the light and close in the dark and when water stress is high in the leaves. When stomata are open, the light intensity on the leaf is the major factor regulating the rate of photosynthesis. Most leaves operate at a maximum rate of photosynthesis if they are in intensities above 20 percent of full sun; below that intensity the rate of photosynthesis drops rapidly, which is why shading of leaves decreases their productivity. Water is required for photosynthesis, but only a very small amount is actually used in the process, and there is always plenty

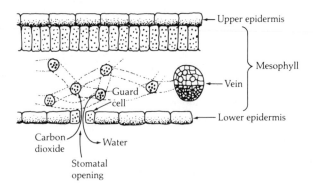

Upper epidermis

Mesophyll

Vein

Guard cell

Lower epidermis

Carbon dioxide

Water

Stomatal opening

16   LEAF STRUCTURE

Leaf cross section showing tissue types and the path of diffusion for water and carbon dioxide during photosynthesis and transpiration. Chloroplasts where photosynthesis occurs are shown as black dots within the mesophyll and guard cells.

of it available. The main effect of water on photosynthesis is that water stress can cause stomata to close and therefore stop the process.

The sugars produced by photosynthesis are translocated in the phloem. The phloem is a living tissue, in contrast to the dead cells in the wood that transport water. The phloem is made by the cambium and is just outside the cambium on the innermost layer of the bark. Sugars are loaded into the phloem at the source and unloaded where they are being used, the sink. Therefore, transport is from source to sink. Loading and unloading are biological processes across the membranes that are the outside limit of the living part of the phloem cells. Except for unloading and loading, sugars cannot pass through the outer cell membranes or else they would leak out of the phloem. Sugars are the major substance moving with the water in the phloem, but there are many other complex substances moving too. The exact mechanism of phloem transport is a subject of controversy, but the theory of mass flow, that water and dissolved substances move together as a solution, has been tested many times and seems to be correct.[1]

Both water and minerals are taken into the tree through the roots from the soil, primarily through the root tips. Obviously the amount of water and nutrients in the soil makes a difference in how much of each can be taken into the roots. As soil moisture decreases, the remaining water is held by the soil particles so that the tendency of the water to move is reduced. This tendency, the free energy of the water, is called *water potential.* Water moves from higher to lower water potential. Water can move from the soil into the roots only if the water potential in the roots is lower than the water potential in the soil. Water potential in the roots is reduced primarily by the tension on the water columns that are pulled up from the roots to the leaves. This tension is commonly called *water stress.* Increased tension on the water columns makes higher water stress and lowers the water potential in the roots to pull water out of the soil.

Nutrients from the soil move to the root dissolved in the water that is being pulled into the roots, but then the dissolved nutrients encounter the membranes around the living cells in the root. Water molecules can pass through the membranes fairly easily, but the nutrient molecules cannot go through membranes with the water. They must be moved through at specific sites by a special biological process that requires energy. This process of nutrient ion uptake is specific for particular nutrients. For instance, potassium ions may be taken into the root while sodium ions are excluded. Nutrients are taken up by mycorrhizal fungi with comparable processes and move through the hyphae of the fungus to the mycorrhizae and then into the tree. Nitrogen is taken into the roots as dissolved nitrate or ammonium and is used in the roots to synthesize amino acids, the building blocks for proteins. Once into the water columns moving up in the wood, the nutrient ions and amino acids move with the water in solution. It is only when they have to pass membranes that ion uptake processes are required, but it is the membranes that cause the rate of nutrient uptake to be different from the rate of water movement.

Although usable nitrogen is scarce in the soil, air is about 80 percent nitrogen. Unfortunately, nitrogen gas is inert and unavailable to most plants. A few plants, and a few trees, have special adaptations to use nitrogen from the air. These trees form root nodules that contain nitrogen-fixing microorganisms. Trees of the legume family, like locust and redbud, have nitrogen-fixing bacteria in their nodules. Nonlegume trees, like alder and Russian olive, have nitrogen-fixing actinomycete fungi. The nitrogen-fixing microorganisms provide usable nitrogen to the tree. Eventually the nitrogen is cycled to other plants as fallen leaves and other organs decay.

Oxygen is necessary for growth. Oxygen is used in respiration, the process where sugars are broken down biochemically to release the energy used in biosynthesis. Oxygen is actually produced by photosynthesis in the leaves, but the rest of the tree must get oxygen from the environment. In most cases oxygen diffuses into each part of the plant either from the air or from dissolved oxygen in the water. The bark of trees has tiny holes, *lenticels*, that permit diffusion into the living cells under the bark. Most roots cannot grow in water without oxygen, but a few, like willows, can tolerate low oxygen or even move oxygen down into the root from aerated portions above.[2]

Valid generalizations about growth regulators are gradually emerging, but for the most part the study of growth regulators is still at the level of case studies of specific examples in a particular part of a plant under a particular set of conditions. Much of the work on growth regulators is not actually done on trees, because trees are so difficult to work with. Usually, results from herbaceous plants are assumed to apply to trees. The major regulators, or classes of regulators, have been identified—although there is always the possibility that there are others that are not yet known. Three classes of regulators generally act to promote various aspects of growth and a fourth class generally inhibits growth. The first regulator is auxin. There seems to be just one active, natural auxin—indole acetic acid—but there are many synthetic compounds with auxin activity. The second class of regulators is made up of the many different natural gibberellins. Each has different levels of activity in different species, but the cheapest to buy and, therefore, the one most used experimentally is gibberellic acid. The third is the cytokinins which were discovered relatively recently. Already several have been identified (the natural cytokinins are expensive, so the synthetic benzyl aminopurine or kinetin are often used experimentally). The inhibitors constitute the fourth and largest class of natural regulatory compounds, but a wide variety are active only in a particular system, and only abscisic acid seems to have a general role in many growth processes in many species. All these regulators are solids that dissolve in water. There is another growth regulator, ethylene, which is a gas that is also soluble in water.

Many details are known about the different growth regulators.[3] Here we can only give a brief summary of their characteristics, but some specific instances will be treated in later chapters. Auxin is produced primarily in shoot tips and leaves, scarcely at all in roots. Gibberellins are produced in shoot and root apical meristems and leaves. Cytokinins are produced in root and shoot apical meristems, but particularly in root apices and also in developing fruit (which is the source of most cytokinins that have been chemically characterized). Abscisic acid is produced in leaves and seeds as well as in other organs. Ethylene is produced particularly by wounded tissue and ripe fruit, but it is also produced more generally within tissues.

Regulators may move up the tree with water in the wood or down the tree with the sugars in the phloem. Auxin has a special, polarized transport system through living cells. Auxin in this polar transport system moves away from the leaves, down to the bottom of the stem, and out toward the root tips. Scarcely any auxin moves in the opposite direction in the polar transport system. Polar transport of auxin seems to be responsible for many of the patterns in the branching systems.

Auxin, gibberellins, and cytokinins generally promote division, enlargement, or some aspect of differentiation, although both auxin and cytokinins may inhibit some processes, especially at relatively high concentrations. Auxin is particularly known for promoting rooting of stem cuttings and is the basis of commercial rooting preparations. There are many synthetic compounds with auxin action, some of which are used to kill weeds and trees or, at lower concentrations, to regulate the dropping of orchard fruits. Applied gibberellins can stimulate extraordinary elongation of shoots. Both gibberellin and cytokinins can break seed dormancy and cause seed germination. Abscisic acid may just generally slow or stop other processes, for instance by causing seed and bud dormancy, but occasionally it promotes a process, as it does in particular in the abscission of leaves and fruits. Ethylene promotes the ripening of fruit, and is the basis of the saying "one rotten apple spoils the barrel" because it is produced by rotting apples and speeds the ripening of the other apples. In many other cases ethylene and auxin effects are closely related because ethylene stimulates auxin formation.

There are many problems associated with studying growth regulators. Most processes are affected by several regulators, rather than just one, and the effects are highly sensitive to the concentrations of the different regulators. A major problem is that most of them are present and effective in plants at concentrations of 0.05 percent or less. Identifying substances at such low concentrations is difficult, tedious, expensive, and all too often inaccurate. Because of the difficulty of studying the regulators actually in the tree, much of our information comes from experiments where natural or synthetic regulators are added to whole trees or parts of trees to study growth. It is even possible to grow small pieces of tissue in test tubes if growth factors are provided and to use this tissue to study the effects of different concentrations and combinations of regulators on subsequent growth of the tissue. By adding the proper regulators at the right concentrations and in the right sequence it is possible to grow roots or shoots from the tissue in a test tube and even to grow a whole new little tree which can subsequently be put in soil and planted outside.

The cell environment, the conditions in which growth occurs, also regulates growth. At many stages of growth there are enzymatic reactions and the rates of these reactions are temperature dependent. Enzyme reactions and growth essentially stop below freezing, reach a maximum between 20 and 30 centigrade (68 to 86 Fahrenheit), and then decrease rapidly at higher temperatures until at around 50 centigrade (140 Fahrenheit) the enzymes are denatured and the cell is killed. Leaves exposed to the direct sun are most in danger of reaching lethal temperatures. In very hot climates leaves are specially designed to stay cool by reflecting light or by dissipating light energy that they have absorbed. One effective design is to have the leaf hang down so that it is not completely in the sunlight. Transpiration of water from leaves cools them because it takes energy to turn water to water vapor, which can evaporate, and this energy is taken from the heat energy in the leaf. Transpiration cools plants the same way that sweating and evaporation of the sweat cools humans.

The problem with transpiration is that if it increases, and if soil moisture is low, then the tension on the water columns increases, and water potential within goes down. The tree goes under water stress. Water potential is another major factor in the environment around a cell. Low water potentials affect practically every physiological process. Low water potential stops cell growth because in order for a cell to enlarge water must move into it from outside the cell, essentially from the water in the water columns. For water to move into the cell, the water potential inside the cell must be lower than the water potential outside the cell. Cells seem to be able to reduce their water potential to a certain point; a point determined by the highest concentration of dissolved substances that they can maintain. As water potential in the water columns drops, first growth stops and then, as water moves out of the cells because of the lower water potential around them, the cells eventually wilt.

Higher leaf temperatures increase transpiration which reduces water potential throughout a tree, but within a tree the water potential also decreases with increasing height.[4] This decrease is created both by the tension needed to hold up a water column as it gets taller and by the tension needed to pull longer water columns through the tiny vessels or tracheids in the wood. Therefore, trees wilt first at the top and dieback of twigs starts at the top. Trees growing in arid areas with low soil moisture and low soil water potential are shorter than those growing in moist areas. A major reason is that the decrease in water potential with height within the tree means that at some height water potential will be too low to permit growth. Assuming that the water potential decreases with height at the same rate in all trees and that growth cannot occur below some minimum water potential, then the maximum height is lower in trees growing on soils with low water potential because the water potential in the roots starts off lower and the decrease with height is the same.

An important and often overlooked aspect of the cell environment is the physical stress on the cells. Cells in tissues are packed together so that each cell contacts many others. Studies of cell shapes have shown that the packing of cells often produces shapes that are very similar to the shapes of soap bubbles packed together in a foam. It is clear that cell differentiation is regulated by the pressures around the cell. Wounds change pressure relations (and also cause ethylene formation) and undifferentiated callus tissue is formed. Not until pressure relations are reestablished do the normal tissues develop in this wound callus. There is also evidence that pressure relations at the apical meristem determine the growth of leaves and other organs.[5] Callus tissue derived from the cambium from trees can be grown in test tubes. C. L. Brown showed that without added pressure on the callus the cells were not elongated, but that when a clamp was put on the callus to simulate the pressure from the bark of an intact tree, the cells that were produced began to elongate and differentiate into cells that were quite similar to wood cells.[6]

ELONGATION OCCURS BY the same basic process in shoots and roots; longitudinal files of cells increase in length through meristematic activity. New cells are added to the files and they subsequently enlarge. The major difference is that shoots produce leaves as they elongate. Elongation separates the leaves that the apical meristem produces so that the leaves do not shade each other. In both roots and shoots, elongation distributes the functional leaves and root tips so that they can then exploit the environment for needed materials.

THE SHOOT SYSTEM

Shoot apical meristems produce stem tissue and lateral leaf primordia. The leaves are attached at nodes and the stem segments between the nodes are internodes. It is helpful to think of the shoot meristem as producing alternating nodes bearing leaf primordia (one per node in alternate-leaved plants and two in opposite-leaved plants) and internodes. Most shoot elongation occurs in the internodes rather than in the nodes.

Once the nodes, with primordia, and the internodes are produced they have a number of possible fates (fig. 17). The primordia may develop either into leaves, cataphylls (much reduced leaves on inhibited shoots), or into bud scales. Bud scales are the highly modified leaves that form the outside of buds. Occasionally in some species an organ halfway between a leaf and a bud

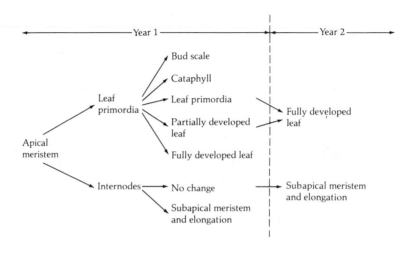

17   FATES OF LEAF PRIMORDIA

scale develops—a bud scale with a small leafy blade. Primordia that develop into leaves may develop part way and then over-winter inside a bud before they complete development, or they may completely develop without any pauses. The internodes are originally formed as short columns of small cells. These inter-nodes may elongate soon after being formed or they may over-winter almost unchanged in a bud along with some partly formed leaves. The following summer some internodes may scarcely elongate (e.g., internodes between bud scales), or they may elongate to varying degrees. Those internodes that elongate sig-nificantly develop subapical, rib meristems that contribute more cells to each radial file. Under natural conditions, if significant internode elongation occurs the major factor determining inter-node length is the amount of activity of the rib meristems.

Trees in temperate climates go through cycles of shoot elonga-tion and bud formation. Buds are really little, compressed shoots made of tiny leaves, nodes, and internodes, that are stored in delayed development. They are protected on the outside by bud scales or by partially developed leaves. The buds wait through bad environmental conditions, like winter or drought, and then the little shoot system expands rapidly under suitable conditions. Preformed leaves allow a tree to produce an effective leaf surface within a few weeks in the spring without having to wait to form new leaves.

Bud formation involves a changing sequence of differentiation of the leaf primordia and internodes produced by the apical meristem. As an example we can look at the extremely simple buds of the opposite-leaved, striped maple (fig. 18). These buds have, from the outside in (or from the bottom to the top): first, a pair of hard, shiny bud scales; then a pair of fuzzy white bud scales; then a pair of preformed leaves a few millimeters long (but with all the pointed lobes already formed); then a pair of conical leaf primordia; and, finally, the apical meristem. In spring the bud scales and preformed leaves begin to elongate as the bud swells before opening. Then the bud opens, the bud scales bend back and fall off, and the preformed leaves rapidly enlarge to form large leaves fifteen centimeters (six inches) or more in diameter. These leaves that grow out so fast are called *early leaves* and they have overwintered in the bud. The pair of conical primordia in the bud develops into bud scales if the shoot is slow growing, or into a second pair of leaves, called *late leaves*, if the shoot is fast growing. Meanwhile, the apical meristem is producing new pairs of leaf primordia and new internodes. In slow-growing shoots, the pair of conical primordia develops into bud scales and there is only one pair of leaves. In fast-growing shoots the conical primordia and one or more of the new pairs of primordia may develop into leaves, but eventually one pair develops into bud scales. Once the first pair of bud scales has developed, then the primordia form, in succession, the second pair of bud scales, then the preformed early leaves, and, finally, the conical pair of leaf primordia on the very inside of the bud so that a new bud is

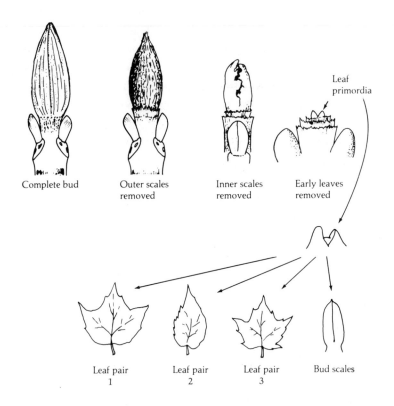

Complete bud | Outer scales removed | Inner scales removed | Early leaves removed

Leaf primordia

Leaf pair 1 | Leaf pair 2 | Leaf pair 3 | Bud scales

18   STRIPED MAPLE BUDS
Bud structure and possible fates of leaf primordia.

formed just like the one that started growing in the spring.

This type of shoot growth is indeterminate. The shoot has the potential of producing an indefinite number of late leaves. Maples, cherries, birches, and poplars are examples of indeterminate species. There are also species with determinate shoots where no late leaves are formed, for instance pines and oaks. Determinate species have only early leaves that were initially formed within a bud. Both determinate and indeterminate species will often produce many late leaves in rapidly growing stump sprouts, the shoots that grow up from the stump of a cut tree. Sometimes these stump sprouts even continue to form new late leaves until the tips are eventually killed by frost in the autumn. Species that are normally determinate, even pines, may be indeterminate as seedlings and can continue leaf production for long periods under good conditions.

Once bud formation is initiated in any species it follows a sequence comparable to that described for striped maple. The major differences are in the numbers of bud scales and early leaves. Most species form larger buds with more early leaves on fast-growing shoots. Pines are determinate species. All the short shoots bearing the leaves are preformed in the bud and shoot elongation can be predicted by the size of the bud.[1] Indeterminate shoots can respond to good conditions of the current season by producing more late leaves. There is also a feedback system operating in determinate species to regulate leaf number according to conditions, but there is usually a year's lag before the shoot can respond to local conditions. Shoots growing under good conditions produce more early leaves and therefore more leaves the next year to take advantage of the good conditions. Leaves growing in shade produce fewer early leaves and therefore grow less the next year. Under deep shade the shoots get progressively smaller until there is not enough leaf surface area to support the shoot and it dies.

In indeterminate species like striped maple, the primordia produced after the early leaves can develop into either leaves or bud scales depending on conditions. Under experimental conditions, if the leaves already formed are in bright light, then successive primordia develop into late leaves, but if the leaves are in shade then the next pair of primordia develop into bud scales. Once the first pair of bud scales is formed, the sequence of bud development is always the same. A second pair of bud scales forms, then the early leaves, and then the undeveloped primordia. However, if the shoot is growing in the shade and the early leaves are cut off, the next pair of primordia develops into leaves rather than bud scales. Also, if the shoot is in the shade and gibberellin is applied to the primordia, they will develop into leaves rather than bud scales. The leaves apparently control the differentiation of the next pair of primordia. In the light they promote leaf development, perhaps by producing gibberellin, in the shade bud scales develop unless the leaves are removed or gibberellin is added. The leaves in the shade may be producing an inhibitor that causes bud-scale differentiation. Removing the leaves removes the inhibitor, so leaves develop. Adding gibberellin overcomes the effect of the inhibitor. There are many unanswered questions. Once bud scales start forming, why do only two pairs form and why does the next pair of primordia differentiate into leaves? How do the bud scales cancel out the effect of the leaves? However it works, it is a very regular and predictable process.

There is a practical result of this control by leaves of primordia differentiation. If leaves are eaten off by insects or animals before a bud has started to form, then more leaves will be made, rather than a bud, and the shoot can continue to photosynthesize. Also, if the early leaves are in the shade then no late leaves are added in a position where they would be unproductive.

In many ways the growth of an internode seems to be regulated by the leaf or leaf pair above it. When buds open, the early leaves grow out before the internodes elongate. Then each late leaf begins to elongate before its associated internode. This lag between leaf and internode development is suggestive that the internode depends on substances from the new leaf for its development. In support of this idea, if the leaves are removed or eaten, the internodes scarcely elongate. In indeterminate hardwoods with long and short shoots, short shoots have only early leaves and short internodes, while long shoots produce late leaves and long internodes. However, even the internodes related to early leaves elongate on late shoots, so it may be that late leaves and long internodes are just both associated with rapid growth, and it is not that late leaves cause long internodes. Sugar maples have an intermediate type of shoot where internodes elongate on shoots with only early leaves.[2]

Much of the plant physiology literature on growth deals with elongation of stems. In general, auxin and gibberellin stimulate stem elongation. Usually both are needed to cause elongation of isolated stem segments. If these regulators are needed, then it seems likely that they come from developing leaves, but if this is so, the problem is to determine why some leaves produce the regulators and others do not.

The sugars needed for shoot elongation early in the spring have to come from stored carbohydrates because the new leaves have not developed enough to be productive. Carbohydrates for new growth are stored primarily in young twigs of deciduous species and in old needles of conifers. Some of the control of shoot development may come from the amount of stored material. Shoots that grew slowly the previous year will have small amounts of stored carbohydrates and therefore will grow slowly, while fast-growing shoots will have more sugars available for early growth.

There are several observations that cast doubt on the generality of the appealing hypothesis that leaves control internode development. In pines, shoot elongation precedes leaf development. The shoots elongate in a few weeks and leaf elongation is not complete for weeks after shoot elongation stops. It seems unlikely that the shoot is controlled by the new leaves, although there are old leaves that might be important. One of the most confusing types of regulation of elongation is the apical control that determines the pattern of new shoot elongation and the decrease in elongation with increasing order number. In the most common pattern of apical control new branches closest to the tip elongate the most and there is progressively less elongation of new branches further from the tip (fig. 19). This pattern has

"Normal"   Apical control
              removed

19   APICAL CONTROL OF BUD DEVELOPMENT

nothing to do with the light intensity on the developing leaves. It is a function of the position of the elongating shoots.

Apical control of shoot elongation is an example of correlative control where an organ—the shoots closer to the tip, in this case—controls the growth of another organ—those shoots further away. Correlative controls are usually thought to utilize growth regulators, and those that are related to position generally involve auxin because it is the only regulator that moves in a single direction so that a pattern can be created. It is easy to prove that apical control is a position effect and not due to inherent differences between the shoots. If the upper stem is cut off, then the buds now at the top develop into long shoots rather than the short shoots they would have been if the upper stem were left intact.

Apical control affects shoot elongation and, in indeterminate shoots, it can cause lower shoots to form bud scales while upper shoots are still forming late leaves, even though both are in the same light intensity. How does apical control of shoot growth and bud formation work? How can another shoot modify the effect of leaves on internode elongation and the fate of leaf primordia? These are good questions without satisfactory answers at present. It certainly seems that the long-distance control must be due to hormones. It seems likely that auxin determines the polarity of the control (from tip to base) and probably gibberellins are involved. It would not be surprising if cytokinins, inhibitors, and, perhaps, ethylene are also involved. The problem of apical control, sometimes called *apical dominance*, has been investigated for almost fifty years by many plant physiologists, and one thing that is clear is that the problem is a lot more complicated than people originally thought.

ELONGATION IN THE ROOT SYSTEM

Elongation in roots is relatively simple compared to elongation in shoots. There are no leaves, nodes, or internodes. There are no buds or bud scales. In fact, roots do not form any real resting structure when they stop growing in the autumn; they just stop. There is only one type of apical meristem, and no subapical meristem. There is no light on the roots, so there are no shading effects.

One major factor controlling the stopping and starting of root growth in temperate zones is the soil temperature. In general, roots will not elongate at temperatures below 4 c (40 f).[3] As winter approaches, the roots stop elongating when soil temperature drops too low. They start again in spring as the soil warms. If the soil stays warm enough, the roots may continue to elongate all year long, even though the stem has stopped growing. A second major factor is drought. Roots will stop growing if the soil is too dry. Roots near the soil surface may stop and start many times during a growth season as the upper soil layers dry out during brief droughts. This drying out is most likely to occur during the middle of the growing season and may be the reason why scientists have observed a reduction in the number of growing root tips during the middle of the summer, which creates a bimodal curve for the number of growing roots that peaks in the spring and the autumn.

The maximum rate of elongation for each tip is correlated to the diameter of the root tip. Woody roots with large diameter root tips (about two mm diameter) may elongate one meter (three feet) in a year, which is more than shoots elongate, while small diameter tips may only elongate one-tenth or one-hundredth that much in a year. There is also apical control as in shoots—the higher-order roots elongate less and have smaller tips.

The relative rate of elongation is determined by a number of soil environment factors. Elongation rate increases as the temperature increases up to an optimum, but temperatures higher than that decrease root elongation and can kill the roots. Forest soil is usually insulated by litter and shaded by the trees above, so soil temperatures seldom exceed the optimum. In the open, the surface soil layers may get very hot and kill any roots that have grown there. Roots elongate fastest in loose soil that offers little resistance and elongation rates decrease as the soil becomes more compacted (as it usually does in the lower soil layers). If soil is very compacted, like a hardpan or soil under a path at a picnic ground, roots cannot penetrate at all unless there are cracks in the soil. Soil moisture can also affect root elongation. Water may slow elongation if there is so much that it decreases the oxygen reaching the roots. Too little soil moisture can decrease elongation by lowering the water potential around the elongating cells.

Roots can be surprisingly independent of shoots. In small seedlings root elongation is very responsive to the activity of the leaves, but in large trees, roots can grow when the shoot system is leafless. Apparently in larger trees, growth factors required from shoots can be stored in the root system. Root elongation depends on photosynthate and vitamins from the shoot system, but little else. Root tips can be cut off and cultured in very simple media that contain only sugar, minerals, and a few vitamins. Roots do not require any added growth regulators for elongation; in fact, many added growth regulators just inhibit root elongation.

There do appear to be situations where root growth and shoot growth control each other in a feedback system that maintains the proper balance of leaf and root surface.[4] If leaf growth exceeds root growth, the rate of water loss through transpiration may exceed the rate of water uptake through the roots, and then the water potential in the leaves goes down. Reduced water potential in the leaves stimulates the formation of abscisic acid, which causes the stomata to close and also slows leaf development. While leaf growth has stopped, root growth continues. As the surface area of the root system increases, more water can be taken up so water potential increases (water stress decreases) in the leaves. The increasing number of roots also increases the amount of gibberellin and cytokinin produced by the root tips that moves up to the shoot system with the water. With raised water potential and higher levels of promoting growth regulators the shoot system begins to grow again and produce more leaves.

NEW APICAL MERISTEMS are formed in specific positions. Lateral shoot apical meristems are formed, with few exceptions, in the axils of leaves. The exceptions are adventitious shoots formed from callus tissue or formed on roots. Lateral root apical meristems are formed, with few exceptions, from the pericycle of roots. The exceptions are adventitious roots formed from callus tissue or parenchyma cells on either roots or shoots. Although each lateral root or shoot apical meristem is basically the same, there can be differences in the size and activity of the meristems right from their initiation. These differences are usually due either to the general vigor of the tree or to the position of the meristems relative to other meristems, another manifestation of apical control. Once formed there can be many different fates of the apical meristems. They may or may not grow at different times, they may even die, and if they do grow they may grow at very different rates.

THE SHOOT SYSTEM

The various possible fates of shoot apical meristems are summarized in figure 20. The first possibilities are either that the new lateral meristem may immediately grow out to form an elongated shoot, called a *sylleptic* shoot, or that it may form a bud. In temperate climates the "normal" thing for new shoot meristems is to form a bud that does not grow out till the following year. In tropi-

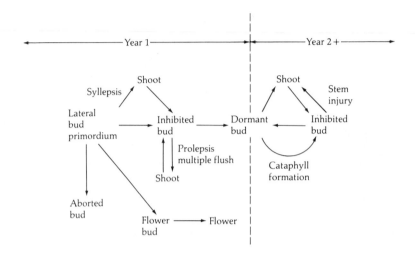

20   FATES OF LATERAL BUDS

cal climates it is "normal" for the lateral meristems to form sylleptic shoots. Some fast-growing individuals of species that usually form buds, for instance, birch and cherry, will form sylleptic shoots in temperate climates. A few temperate species like alder and sweetgum regularly form sylleptic shoots. Why in some fast-growing birches and such do some lateral meristems grow out to form sylleptic shoots? Usually the meristems that grow out are a group associated with the first few late leaves, but the rest of the laterals stay inhibited till the next year (fig. 21). Shoots from rapidly growing stump sprouts often develop sylleptic lateral branches toward the base. Incidentally, these sylleptic shoots do not grow out in the usual pattern of long shoots at the top and short shoots at the bottom. Instead, the pattern is reversed and the lower older shoots are the longest. Apical control does not seem to work in sylleptic shoots.

Most lateral apical meristems eventually form buds whether or not there is an intervening period of sylleptic shoot growth. Some

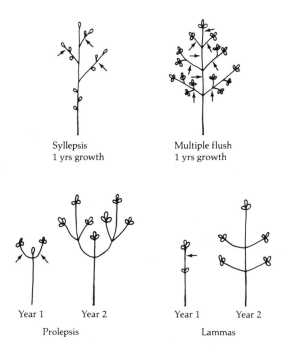

Syllepsis
1 yrs growth

Multiple flush
1 yrs growth

Year 1   Year 2

Prolepsis

Year 1   Year 2

Lammas

21   UNUSUAL BUD GROWTH
Arrows indicate shoots from buds that grew out the year they were
formed.

trees, like eucalypts, have many shoots that never form buds,
although they may pause in growth during inhospitable environmental conditions. In these species the apical meristems and
young leaves are protected by the enclosing older leaves.

If a lateral shoot meristem forms a bud immediately, the bud is
inhibited from growing by other parts of the plant. If the leaves
are removed, or if the stem is injured above the bud, although the
lateral bud is inhibited it will grow out to form a shoot. Buds on
vigorous trees may overcome the inhibition and grow out as a result of favorable environmental conditions. There are three different types of such growth. There may be a multiple flush where
the terminal and laterals grow out one or more times during

a growing season (see fig. 21). Fast-growing southern pines have several flushes of growth, often four to six in a year. At each flush the terminal elongates, a new whorl of lateral branches is formed, and new buds are formed. This sequence of flushes makes it difficult for people who are used to northern pines, which form only one whorl of branches each year, to determine the age of a tree by simply counting the number of annual whorls of branches. It still may be possible to determine the age of southern pines by counting whorls because the first flush each year usually produces the greatest terminal elongation and successive flushes elongate less so that there is an annual repeating pattern of long to short flushes.

Fast-growing individuals of many temperate species that do not have multiple flushes will briefly resume growth after making buds if the early summer weather is warm and moist. This extra growth is usually much less than the previous elongation in the spring. Often just the terminal grows (*lammas growth*), or just the laterals grow (*prolepsis*) (see fig. 21). Lammas growth looks odd because it is so much less than a normal year's growth, but it does not drastically affect the form of the tree. Prolepsis is particularly common in fast-growing pines. The lateral buds grow out in the same year they are formed, but the terminal does not. In following years these precocious laterals frequently dominate the terminal shoot and several of the lateral branches may become replacement terminals. The result is a much-forked main stem that closely resembles the forking resulting from injury to the main stem. Such injuries are particularly common from the white pine weevil in the eastern United States. The insect tends to attack trees growing in the open. Usually the much-forked form of "pasture pines" is attributed to the effect of the weevil, but in young, fast-growing trees the results of prolepsis are nearly identical and are most likely to occur in open fields where growth is rapid. Prolepsis can be distinguished from weevil damage because there is no dead terminal and because there is a small whorl of branches on each proleptic shoot near the point of forking.

When these various episodes of growth are finished and winter approaches, the buds gradually become dormant in addition to being inhibited. As the buds go deeper into dormancy they reach a stage where they will not grow even if the stem is injured or if growing conditions are perfect. In most temperate species dormant buds will not grow until they have met their chilling requirement by being exposed for some minimum time to temperatures near freezing.

When buds have received the necessary cold treatment they may then grow out under favorable conditions in the spring. As discussed in the section on elongation, when no lateral buds grow out the year they are formed, the following year the uppermost buds elongate the most and the lowermost, the least. Where there is a difference between long and short shoots, the long shoots are uppermost and there are more of them in fast-growing, vigorous trees. For instance, fast-growing pines have more branches in each whorl than do slow-growing pines. The same principle holds for hardwoods that do not have as clear-cut differences between long and short shoots and so there are more long shoots on vigorous trees. Thus the amount of growth of a particular lateral is determined both by bud position and by overall vigor of the parent shoot.

The ultimate effect of position on growth of buds is that the lowermost buds on hardwoods may not grow out at all. They may abort and fall off or they may grow very slowly, at the same rate that the stem is enlarging radially. The lateral buds associated with bud scales are a good example of buds that grow slowly. These slow-growing shoots are some of the reserve buds that grow out after injury to form epicormic shoots or stump sprouts. As they grow extremely slowly, mostly hidden in the bark, they produce much-reduced scales instead of leaves and they occasionally branch. Because they branch, the number of these reserve buds increases and there can be hundreds of them at the base of a hardwood tree. It is this large number of reserve buds that permits trees to sprout and resprout when the stem is cut off.

The inhibition of bud outgrowth by the shoot above is called apical dominance. Apical dominance determines whether a bud will grow out, apical control (discussed in chap. 6) regulates how much the bud grows once it has started. These two closely related, correlative controls determine the annual patterns of shoot development. Although they are probably manifestations of the same control system, it is useful to separate the two controls because they happen at different times in shoot development. Apical dominance can be viewed as the ultimate expression of apical control where shoot growth is so restricted that no detectable shoot is formed.

Apical dominance when new lateral meristems are formed causes the meristems to form buds. Once the sequence of bud formation is initiated the bud scales themselves tend to keep the early leaves from developing in the bud. The key control is to start the leaf primordia differentiating into bud scales and then the process is self-regulating. Removing leaves or injuring the terminal shoot early in the summer removes the apical dominance of lateral buds and they grow out to form shoots. Later in the season, injury will not permit shoot development because the buds are dormant. Therefore, at least early in bud development, the internal inhibition in the lateral bud is not enough to keep it from growing out, but the correlative inhibition from above does inhibit shoot formation. The inhibition can be largely replaced in de-topped stems by applying auxin to the stem above the bud. In some cases the correlative inhibition can be broken by applying cytokinins directly to the inhibited bud. As in apical control, the actual mechanism of apical dominance is not clear. It probably involves several growth regulators and is modified by the general growth rate of the plant.

Cases like multiple flush, where shoots grow out and form

buds which grow out again in the same year, are different from apical dominance and control yet they share some features. Here both laterals and terminals may be affected so the control is not polar, it does not just come from leaves or buds above. Apparently the buds are not totally self-inhibited because they can grow out, but they need good general conditions to do so. Perhaps the good conditions change the ratio of various growth regulators produced by leaves and roots enough to permit buds that are still developing to grow out before they become dormant.

Abortion occurs in some of the lower lateral buds each year, but there also are many species whose terminal buds abort each year. Perhaps it would be more accurate to say the terminal portion of the growing shoot aborts each year. When this happens, the role of the terminal is taken the next year by the uppermost lateral bud, called in this instance a *pseudoterminal* bud. Elms, birches, chestnuts, sycamores, locusts, and basswoods are examples of trees that have pseudoterminal buds. Every year on every growing shoot the terminal portion aborts and a lateral takes over the next year. This type of growth produces characteristically zigzag twigs. All these trees mentioned above have alternate leaves, but a few species with opposite leaves, for example cork tree and the shrub bladdernut, also have terminal bud abortion. As a result, the uppermost pair of laterals grows out and tends to cause a fork in the stem the next year.

Terminal-shoot abortion is not just death of the terminal; it is an active physiological process of abscission similar to the shedding of leaves in autumn. A special layer of cells, an abscission zone, develops across the stem. The bonding between the cells in the zone weakens and eventually the shoot breaks off at the abscission zone. The process apparently occurs in response to decreasing day lengths because it can be prevented by growing plants under artificial long days.

If a tree has reached maturity and is capable of flowering, shoot meristems may develop into flower meristems. In trees only a small proportion of the meristems becomes flowers. As in apical control and dominance, the position of the meristem is important in determining its fate. Flowers usually form from lateral meristems. These may be concentrated on small lateral branches like the spur shoots of apple trees. In red maples, and some other maples, extra lateral flower buds develop at the lower nodes on fast-grown shoots so that each node (a pair of leaf scars and associated buds) has six or more flower buds. Occasionally flower buds are terminal buds. Terminal flowers occur regularly in some shrubs such as staghorn sumac. We have observed frequent terminal flower formation in the lower, slow-growing branches of striped maple.

The position of flower buds affects form because development of a flower bud uses up all of the meristem. When the flower, or fruit, eventually falls off there is no meristem for continued growth. As a result, spur shoots in fruit trees do not branch because the lateral meristems become flowers. Terminal flowering usually results in forking of the stem the next year, just as though the terminal bud had aborted. The terminal meristem is lost, apical control is lost, and several laterals grow out rapidly. Forking marks the point of flowering in staghorn sumac and in striped maples. The forking remains as a record of the flowering of previous years.

The position of meristems may determine not only whether a bud becomes a flower, but, particularly in some conifers, the sex of the flower as well. (Technically, the sex of the cone is what will be determined because conifers do not have flowers.) In pines, the female cones develop at the top of the tree and the male cones, at the bottom. In Douglas-fir the cones develop from lateral buds on elongating branches. The female cones develop toward the tip of the branch and the male cones toward the base.

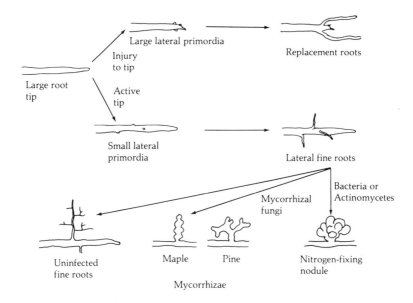

Large lateral primordia

Injury
to tip

Replacement roots

Large root
tip

Active
tip

Small lateral
primordia

Lateral fine roots

Mycorrhizal
fungi

Bacteria or
Actinomycetes

Uninfected
fine roots

Maple   Pine

Nitrogen-fixing
nodule

Mycorrhizae

22   FATES OF ROOT TIPS

THE ROOT SYSTEM

The possible fates of apical root meristems are relatively limited
compared to the possible fates of shoot meristems (fig. 22). One
important factor determining the fate of root meristems is their
initial size. Lateral ,root meristems are usually relatively small,
whether they are formed on large or small root tips. Small meristems grow out to form small-diameter tips and small, fine roots.
These small meristems are formed some distance behind the parent tips. Because lateral root tips are smaller than their parent
tips, root-tip diameter generally decreases with increasing order
number. If the root tip is injured, however, then the lateral root
meristems form just behind the injury and they are about the size
of the injured parent tip. If a large-diameter root tip is injured,
large-diameter lateral tips develop. These large-diameter laterals

bend to go in the same general direction as the parent tip and, if there are more than one, the result is a fork in the root system.

It seems that the root system also has a sort of apical dominance and control. When the terminal meristem is active, the laterals that form are small and at some distance from the tip. When the terminal is removed the lateral meristems form close to the end of the root and they are much larger. The activity of the tip appears to determine the position, relative size, and direction of growth of the lateral meristem. Auxin from the stem is required for the initiation of lateral roots.[1] Root tips produce a number of growth regulators: gibberellins, cytokinins, and abscisic acid. These regulators from the tip and the ones from the stem must interact somehow. Regulators from the root tip appear to inhibit the process of lateral initiation and development, causing the lateral primordia to occur at a distance from the tip and reducing the size of the meristem formed.

The biggest change in root tips occurs in response to infection from other organisms.[2] Roots of almost all tree species form mycorrhizae after infection by the hyphal strands of underground fungi. Roots of a relatively few tree species form nitrogen-fixing nodules after they are infected by bacteria or by tiny, actinomycete fungi. Both mycorrhizae and nitrogen-fixing nodules are physiologically important. Mycorrhizae help the tree by accumulating nutrients, particularly phosphate, that the roots could not otherwise get. Nitrogen-fixing nodules permit trees to get nitrogen, generally the scarcest nutrient, directly from the air so that they can survive in nitrogen-poor soils. Trees with nitrogen-fixing nodules tend to grow in infertile areas like sands, gravel, or bogs. They are valuable for planting on areas like road banks and strip mines that have nutrient-deficient soils.

Slow-growing, small, high-order roots form mycorrhizae. Because most of the roots in a large root system are small and high order, there are vast numbers of mycorrhizae. The hyphal strands of the fungi grow in the soil. There are two types of mycorrhizae. In one the fungal strands are mostly outside the cells of the root. The hyphae form a mantle around the outside of the root and grow between cells, although a few hyphae penetrate the cells. These mycorrhizae in pines can be identified because they are short, relatively thick, and, frequently, forked. The other kind of mycorrhizae have hyphae that proliferate inside the cells of the root with very few hyphae on the outside. Maple roots develop these mycorrhizae, which look like a chain of beads (see fig. 22). Not all mycorrhizae look different from uninfected roots on the outside, but many kinds are swollen because the cells of the outer layers of the root enlarge when they are infected. Mycorrhizae may also lack root caps.

One group that forms nitrogen-fixing nodules is the legumes, the pea family. There are relatively few temperate, leguminous trees; locusts and redbud are examples, but there are more tropical representatives. The nodules form when the bacteria enter the root through a root hair. There is a complex process where the plant actually builds a special internal structure around the bacteria. The bacteria then multiply within the cells of the root. The nodules are swollen, short, and contain a substance closely related to the hemoglobin in our blood. Other plants form nitrogen-fixing nodules with single-celled actinomycete fungi. These plants are not limited to one family. Casuarinas are widespread subtropical trees. Alder is a widespread genus of trees and shrubs that grows north to the Arctic. Sweet gale, a shrub that grows in acid bogs, is another example. There are fourteen genera in seven different nonleguminous families that form nitrogen-fixing nodules. The infection process is somewhat comparable to bacterial invasion of legume roots. The structure of the two types of nodules is superficially the same, but actinomycete nodules lack the hemoglobinlike compound.

8 : Thickening from cambial activity

CAMBIAL ACTIVITY THICKENS the framework produced by elongation and lateral formation. The products of cambial activity—wood and phloem—are most of the tree's bulk. The products of apical meristems are only a millimeter or two in diameter, but the trunk of a large tree may be several meters thick. Most of the biomass in a forest is wood that accumulates from cambial activity. The phloem is just as necessary as wood in the function of a tree, but because there is not nearly so much of it and because its cell walls are relatively thin and unlignified, phloem does not accumulate a tremendous amount of biomass.

Wood is added to the framework of the tree in sheaths just underneath the bark. The sheaths are added as if the tree were putting on successive pairs of long underwear—adding each layer on top of the last and getting fatter and fatter as each new sheath is produced. Usually we see these sheaths in a tree only from cross sections of branches, stem, or roots. In cross section each layer looks like a ring. In temperate areas, rings are usually annual, but in other areas there may be more than one growth ring in a year or, in many tropical trees, there may be no distinguishable rings at all.

There are three common types of wood: coniferous wood (softwood), ring-porous wood, and diffuse-porous wood (both hardwoods) (fig. 23). All wood is made mostly of vertically oriented cells for strength, water conduction, and, perhaps, some storage. There are also horizontally oriented cells, the ray cells, that conduct materials radially into the wood from the outer parts of the

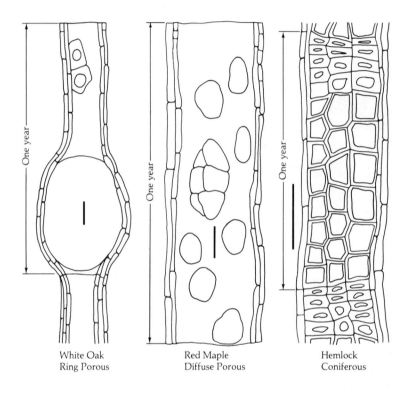

White Oak
Ring Porous

Red Maple
Diffuse Porous

Hemlock
Coniferous

23   WOOD TYPES

A portion of cross sections of annual rings showing rays and the water-conducting cells (vessels in oak and maple, tracheids in hemlock). The hemlock drawing is magnified twice as much as the other types (the bar in each drawing is 0.1 mm long).

Phloem   Xylem

Sieve Cell   Tracheid

                                          Fiber

Sieve Tube Element

                                          Vessel

Parenchyma   Fusiform
              Cambial Cell   Parenchyma

Phloem   Ray Cambial   Xylem
Ray Cell   Cell   Ray Cell

24 DIFFERENTIATION OF CAMBIAL CELLS
Sieve cells and sieve tube members are specialized for phloem transport; vessels are specialized for water transport, as fibers are for strength; tracheids combine specialization for both strength and water transport; parenchyma often store materials; ray cells transport materials radially (e.g., from the phloem into the wood).

tree (fig. 24). Ray cells are aggregated into the rays that are often visible as lines on the surface of finished wood, particularly oak. Individual ray cells are somewhat similar in different wood types, but rays are smaller in softwoods than in hardwoods. Generally rays constitute 10–30 percent of the wood volume. The vertical cells of different wood types are quite different, one from another. Coniferous wood is made almost entirely of tracheids, small needle-shaped (*fusiform*) cells a few millimeters long and twenty to forty microns wide (1,000 microns equal 1 millimeter). Tracheids serve both to strengthen the wood with their thick walls and to conduct water through their hollow interiors. Water

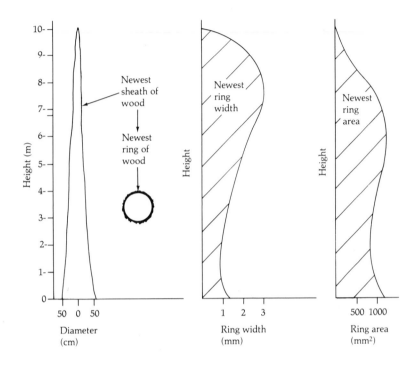

25   WOOD DISTRIBUTION
Distribution of an annual sheath of wood on a tree stem.

longitudinal parenchyma → passes from tracheid to tracheid through holes in the walls called pits. There may also be occasional fusiform parenchyma in coniferous wood to store materials. Hardwoods have developed a division of labor in vertical wood cells. Cells vary in shape, yet they all were derived from similar fusiform cambial cells. Vessels are made of tubelike elements lined up vertically to provide efficient channels for water transport. Thick-walled fibers are specialized for strength and thin-walled parenchyma for storage. Diffuse-porous wood has vessels forty to sixty microns wide scattered throughout the wood. Ring-porous wood has a ring of very large vessels produced at the beginning of each annual ring and a few small vessels in the rest of the ring. These large vessels may be over 300 microns wide and just visible to the unaided eye. Ring-porous wood represents the ultimate in specialization of cell types. The large vessels are very efficient in water transport, but there are relatively few of these vessels so the system is risky if the large vessels become nonfunctional.

The ring width of the annual sheath of cambial activity varies from the top to the bottom of the tree.[1] The ring width changes according to the position of the ring in relation to the crown of the tree. The most-recent annual ring in a tree, the ring at the outside just under the bark, is smallest near the top of the tree, largest toward the base of the crown where the most productive branches are, and gradually smaller going down the tree below the live crown (fig. 25). Usually the ring width increases right at the base of the tree where the major lateral roots are attached to the stem. There are differences in distribution of ring width according to the size and distribution of the live crown. Very suppressed trees with very short crowns may not even grow near the base of the tree, although they cannot survive long if they grow that slowly. Open-grown trees with live crowns nearly to the bottom may have increasing ring width right to the base of the stem.

The inherent pattern of ring width within any annual sheath is determined by the position and vigor of the crown. This pattern of cambial activity is reflected in an inherent pattern of ring widths in any given cross section going from the pith in the center to the bark on the outside. The ring next to the pith was formed at the top of the tree, the part of the tree that is only one year old. The next ring was formed in the two-year-old portion of the top of the tree, the third ring from the pith in the three-year-old portion of the top, and so forth. Any one cross section stays in the same place relative to the ground, but every year as the terminal shoots elongate, the section gets further and further away from the top of the tree. Eventually it will be where the most productive branches are and then later it will be below the crown. Thus, the pattern from pith to bark in a section reflects the pattern from tip to base of the tree within any one sheath of wood.

The sum of all the annual sheaths of wood determines the form of the stem of the tree. Open-grown trees have ring widths increasing from top to bottom, so when they are added together the stem tapers all the way from top to bottom. Forest-grown trees, where ring width decreases below the crown, have stems that taper within the crown, but that may be almost cylindrical below the crown.

In the root system, ring widths decrease exponentially with distance from the stem in mature trees.[2] This decrease produces a zone of rapid taper within one to two meters (three to six feet) of the stem. In that zone, ring widths are much greater on the top of the root than on the underside. Beyond the zone of rapid taper, ring widths are narrow all around the root and decrease very slightly with increasing distance from the stem. The roots stay about the same diameter and are almost ropelike until there is a major fork in the root. The annual rings in these roots are frequently discontinuous and they do not extend all the way around the root. Discontinuities make it difficult to determine the age of roots by counting rings.

We frequently make judgments about the rate of cambial activity based on the ring width. For instance, if the rings are wider inside the tree than at the outside it seems that the tree is slowing in growth. However, the actual amount of cambial activity, the total area of wood produced each year, may be increasing even though the ring width is decreasing (see fig. 25). The area of a ring of constant width increases with distance from the center of the tree because the circumference of the tree increases. The influence of the increasing circumference can offset the effect of decreasing ring widths. If a tree is maintaining a constant ring width at a cross section then it must actually be producing more wood at that section each year.

Cambial activity starts at about the same time in all the trees of a species in a stand whether they are fast- or slow-growing. The stimulus is the combination of the longer days and warmer temperatures of spring. All indications are that cambial activity is controlled primarily by growth regulators coming from leaves and growing buds. The initiation of cambial activity starts below newly active buds in diffuse-porous and coniferous trees. Cambial activity then spreads down the trunk at five to ten cm per hour, which is approximately the rate of polar auxin transport. If the stem is girdled by removing a band of bark and phloem below the expanding buds then the wave of initiation is stopped and there is no cambial activity below the girdle. Experiments with isolated stem segments from which the buds were removed show that adding auxin and gibberellin to the top end of the section initiates almost normal cambial activity.[3] Auxin alone causes a few cells to differentiate and gibberellin alone causes the production of cells which do not differentiate. Together the two regulators stimulate both division and differentiation.

Ring-porous trees start cambial activity before the buds grow and activity starts all over the tree at about the same time. It is important for cambial activity to proceed before the leaves grow out in ring-porous trees because the new leaves depend on the new vessels for water. Apparently cambial activity starts in ring-porous trees because an auxin precursor from the leaves was stored in the cambial zone the previous autumn.[4] In the spring, according to the theory, the precursor is converted to auxin and the auxin initiates cambial activity, but there is no wave of initiation because the precursor is distributed throughout the tree and is converted at about the same time throughout the tree.

Once cambial activity has been initiated it still needs regulators from above to continue. The rate of activity may vary and the rate can be measured by the rate of cell production. The rate of cell production is determined by the number of dividing cells in each file and the rate at which they divide. In white spruce the rate is determined primarily by the number of dividing cells and the rate of division is similar for fast- and slow-growing trees.[5] In other species both the number of dividing cells and the rate of division may vary. It is not known which regulators determine either the rate of division or the number of dividing cells.

Cessation of cambial activity seems to occur as the production of regulators by leaves slows and stops, although there is always the possibility of inhibitors building up in the cambial zone toward the end of the season. In pines, cambial activity stops shortly after needle elongation stops, but needle elongation proceeds long after the cessation of shoot elongation. In diffuse-porous trees, which are usually indeterminate so that their shoot growth may continue for some time, cambial activity also stops shortly after the leaves stop growing. In ring-porous trees, which are usually determinate species whose leaves stop growing early in the season, cambial activity continues after leaf growth in fast-growing trees, presumably because the mature leaves continue to produce growth regulators. In general, cambial activity stops first at the base of the tree, then up the stem, and finally in the crown.

Although initiation of cambial activity occurs at about the same time in trees of different growth rates, cessation usually occurs earlier in slow-growing, suppressed trees than in fast-growing, dominant trees. Variation in ring width between trees is, therefore, due both to differences in rate of cell production during cambial activity and to the length of time that the cambium is active during a season. The same factors that produce different ring widths between trees probably also determine the different ring widths up and down an annual sheath of wood in any one tree. Cambial activity goes on for a longer time in the crown, because it starts in the crown and stops first toward the base, but the rate of cell production may also be faster in the crown because there is a higher concentration of growth regulators there.

It is clear that the position of the cambium relative to the crown, which is the source of both growth regulators and photosynthate, is a major determinant of annual ring width. The nearer the cambium to the most active leaves, the wider the annual ring. The swaying of the stem in the wind is another important factor in regulating ring width. If a tree sways back and forth so that the stem is bent frequently, then wood is added to the stem to keep the actual bending at the surface of the cambium the same along the whole length of the stem.[6] If a particular part of the stem bends more, then it will have more cambial activity and, as a result, the amount of bending will be reduced because the stem becomes stronger. This sort of feedback between bending and cambial activity occurs constantly along the whole stem as it sways. If a stem is stopped from swaying by guying it with wires, cambial activity is reduced even though photosynthesis is unaffected in the short term by the guying.[7] There are some practical effects of the stimulation of cambial activity by stem sway. If newly planted street trees are supported by guy wires for too long, the stem below the wires will not thicken enough to support the tree when the wires are finally removed and it will break in the wind. Trees in dense plantations are restricted from swaying because the crowns are in such close contact. As a result the lower stems are relatively thin. When the stand is thinned the trees are suddenly exposed to the wind. Many of them break if there is a wind storm before the stems have had time to respond to the increased amount of sway by thickening the lower portion of the stem.

Growth rings in the wood are marked by differences in cell size and cell-wall thickness. In conifers the first-formed tracheids (the *earlywood*) have relatively large diameters and thin walls, and the last-formed tracheids (the *latewood*) have relatively small diameters and thick walls. In Douglas-fir the actual amount of wall produced in each cell is the same in both early and late wood, but, because the cells are smaller in late wood, the walls are thicker.[8] Most conifers have rings that are easily seen and counted, primarily because the dense latewood is darker brown as a result of its high lignin content. It can be shown experimentally in pines that cell size (radial diameter) and cell-wall thickness are under separate controls. Trees grown under artificial long days can produce "long-day latewood," large-diameter cells with thick walls. Under drought conditions trees may produce drought rings, with small-diameter, thin-walled cells in the latewood.[9] One theory is that auxin concentration regulates tracheid diameter. Auxin concentration is high in the spring and summer so diameters are large, but auxin decreases later in the year and thus the cells are smaller in diameter. Recent careful measurements have shown that auxin concentration is higher in the spring in the cambial zone of pine,[10] but other regulators are probably also involved. Wall thickness largely reflects the amount of available photosynthate. Trees grown under high night temperatures have high levels of respiration at night, high use of photosynthate, and thus produce thin-walled cells. Trees grown under low night temperatures have lower respiration rates, more available photosynthate, and thicker walls.[11] Another factor in wall thickness may be that latewood cells stay alive longer and therefore have more time to synthesize new walls.

Diffuse-porous wood has rings that are hard to see. The latewood is only marked by a few small fibers that are not highly lignified. If you are trying to determine the age of trees by counting rings, avoid diffuse-porous species like maple, cherry, and birch because the rings are so hard to count. Instead, select either a conifer (hemlock is easy to count) or a ring-porous tree like an oak. Ring-porous trees have very obvious rings because of the large vessels in the first-formed earlywood. These vessels are presumably so large because they form during the initial period when there is a high level of auxin present following conversion of the auxin precursor. After this first band of wood with large cells the rest of the earlywood has very few vessels and the latewood is no more distinguishable than in diffuse-porous trees.

Cell types in diffuse-porous and ring-porous woods are distributed in a regular pattern for each species. The pattern is so characteristic that it is a major feature in identifying wood. Vessels, or groups of vessels, are spaced fairly regularly within the matrix of fibers. Parenchyma are usually in some predictable position relative to the vessels, often just around them. Not only are the cell types in a regular pattern in cross sections, but there also is vertical continuity of development so that vessel elements are lined up to make the vertical, continuous files that form the vessels.

These complex geometric patterns of cell distribution are probably determined by growth regulators. The pattern of cell formation can be totally changed by applying growth regulators. High auxin concentrations can produce wood that is almost all vessels, high gibberellin can produce wood that is mostly parenchyma. In experiments with ash, a ring-porous wood, the number of sites that form the large vessels in the spring can be modified by changing the gibberellin concentration, but the number of vessels formed at each site is controlled by auxin. [12] The vertical control of vessel development seems to be from auxin moving down from the leaves. Once a vessel has started to differentiate it appears to interact with the adjoining cells to maintain spacing between vessels and to cause parenchyma to develop in predictable positions relative to the vessels. The enlarging vessels either could be producing substances that regulate differentiation of the other cells or could be using up some factor required for vessel differentiation. The whole process of regulation of wood development is complex because it occurs in four dimensions, the three spatial dimensions and the time dimension. All this takes place in a narrow layer just outside the cambial zone.

Dead trees, where the bark has fallen off, often show spiral grain. The cells, and the cracks that form between the cells as wood dries or is split, actually run at an angle to the stem and spiral around it. The grain angle often changes over time and even may change from spiraling to the left to spiraling to the right. An elegant way to demonstrate these changes in grain angle is with

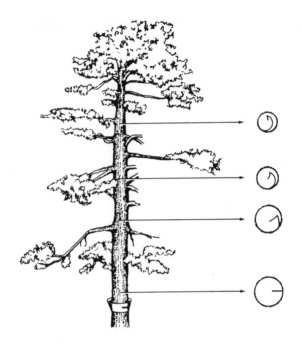

26   DYE ASCENT
The dye is put in a collar around the stem and the leaves pull it into a hole
drilled in the wood. As the dye moves up the stem it follows the path of
spiral grain and the movement to the side is shown in cross sections
taken at different heights.

a dye ascent. [13] In this process, a hole is drilled deep into the wood
at the base of a transpiring tree and dye from a reservoir is pulled
into the wood and up the tree. At each point along the length of
the hole the dye moves up in the direction of the grain. If the grain
spirals to the right the dye will be displaced to the right, and vice
versa for a left-handed spiral. The path of movement of the dye
can be followed by cutting the tree down and taking out disks at
intervals up the stem (fig. 26). The history of the changes in orientation of the grain from the inside, the past, to the outside,
the present, is revealed by the relative displacement around the

stem. In trees with interlocked grain where the wood is hard to split, like elm, the grain may change from a right- to a left-handed spiral each year. In many trees the grain angle reverses after a few years and gradually increases over the years so that spiral grain angle is greater in older than younger trees. One of the best ways to become interested in grain angle and to study it first hand is to split firewood. Working with firewood makes one really appreciate straight-grained wood that splits with a touch of an axe as opposed to interlocked grain, as in elm, where it is possible to bury a wedge in the wood and hardly split it at all. Another subject of practical study is the distortions of grain around knots or at branches, which makes splitting difficult.

Spiral grain originates in the cambial zone. It has to be formed there because wood cells cannot change orientation once they have developed thick walls. The probable cause is that when fusiform initial cells divide perpendicularly to form new files of cells (a *pseudotransverse division*) the new cell wall is slanted across the parent fusiform initial. Whole areas of cambium may have the new slanted walls predominantly in one direction.[14] After the pseudotransverse divisions the daughter cambial cells slowly elongate at the tips. If the direction of the new walls is random then the direction of the grain stays the same, but if the direction of the new walls is predominantly one way, the grain angle will gradually change. In some trees the areas where divisions are predominantly in one direction slowly move over the surface of the cambium so that the grain changes irregularly; in others the change is more regular. Changes in grain angle are not clearly related to structural demands of the stem.

Once wood is formed, the water-transporting cells die quite rapidly, but parenchyma cells and ray cells may live for decades. Younger wood toward the outside of the tree is functional in water transport. This light-colored wood is called *sapwood*. Older wood, the *heartwood*, becomes nonfunctional in water transport. The vessels are filled with air and may then be blocked by ingrowths (*tyloses*) from parenchyma cells. As the vessels and tracheids become nonfunctional, materials are transported down the rays and stored in the heartwood. These materials often combine to form the dark-colored substances that make it easy to differentiate heartwood. It seems likely that the heartwood is being used as a chemical dump for the excretion of unwanted substances. One of the results is our finest cabinet woods, which in fact are the attractively colored heartwoods from the tree's waste disposal system.

THE PRECEDING CHAPTERS have discussed how
the framework of the tree is built by apical meristems producing
new axes in regular patterns and how the framework is then
thickened by cambial activity. This information, along with the
information on how the different axes are attached to each other,
is almost sufficient to describe the structure of a tree. What is
needed to complete the description is information about the orientation of each axis and how that orientation changes over time
if an axis moves. The orientation of apical growth determines the
initial position of axes. There may be later movements due to
bending from self-weight or bending from special wood called
reaction wood.

Orientation of an axis can be described in relation to the vertical, using angles and a three-dimensional coordinate system, or
in relation to the parent axis from which it was derived, using angles alone. Both methods have some virtue. Axes oriented with
respect to gravity (vertical) are best described in a coordinate system because to some extent the axes orient independently of each
other. On the other hand, many aspects of axis orientation are not
independent. For instance, if a tree is tipped over or swayed in
the wind, the same basic orientation is kept between axes, but
every axis changes orientation within a coordinate system.

The first axes of a tree are the primary root and shoot growing
out of the seed. The root grows down and the shoot grows up. All
the rest of the axes of a tree originate laterally as lateral meristems. The initial orientation of each lateral is determined by its

angle relative to its parent axis and its position around the parent axis. If a lateral grows at right angles to a horizontal parent axis, it will grow up if it starts on the top, horizontally if it starts on the side, and down if it starts on the bottom.

Once a lateral has started to elongate, it may change orientation by differential stem elongation just behind the apical meristem. If the stem elongates more on one side than the other it causes curved growth. Presumably differential growth occurs because of a differential distribution of growth regulators. Auxin is the regulator usually implicated. Once the cells have differentiated, they can no longer cause curved growth and changes in orientation. Any further changes in orientation due to growth occur from cambial activity, which will be discussed in the next chapter. Orientation may also be changed by passive bending from self-weight, except for roots supported in the soil, or by changes in orientation of parent axes, for instance, when a tree is tipped over.

Differential growth movements in response to some stimulus are called *tropisms*. The stimulus causes differential distribution of growth regulators and thus differential growth. Geotropism is a growth movement in response to the stimulus of gravity. Positive geotropism is differential growth to grow down and negative geotropism is differential growth to grow up. The best examples of geotropism are seedling roots and shoots. If a germinating seed is tipped, the root bends to keep growing down and the shoot bends to keep growing up. Another tropism is phototropism, growing toward (positive) or away from (negative) the light. If the light is moved the axis grows toward, or away from, the new position of the light. Seedling shoots are positively phototropic and bend toward the light, but phototropism is not important in shoots of larger trees.

It is not always safe to interpret the distribution of roots or shoots in terms of tropisms. For instance, when a tree grows up in the shade of a taller tree, the crown of the small tree may appear to be growing out toward the light, away from the overhead shade. It is possible that this uneven crown development toward the light represents phototropism, but it is far more likely that the branches on the better-lit side of the crown survived and grew relatively rapidly while the branches on the shaded side grew slowly or died. The result of better growth on one side than the other is an apparent tropism, not a real tropism. Another example of an apparent tropism is when roots are clogging sewer pipes. It is tempting to think that the roots responded to the presence of the sewer pipe and grew toward it, but actually what happened is that one or two roots happened to grow into the pipe where the conditions were so favorable that they proliferated and clogged the pipe.

ORIENTATION IN THE SHOOT SYSTEM

Lateral buds are inserted at an angle on the parent axis, usually from thirty to sixty degrees. In many cases the terminal buds on the end of lateral branches are inserted at an angle to the rest of the parent axis, usually pointing more upward. Buds initially grow out at the insertion angle, but after that, different species behave differently. In some species, like spruces, the branches just continue to grow out at the same angle as the insertion angle. In many hardwoods the elongating lateral shoot bends upward but usually not all the way to vertical unless the insertion angle was near vertical. As the leaves develop, their weight tends to bend the new shoots downward.

In pines, all the shoots initially bend to grow straight up while they are elongating. During this stage the light-colored vertical shoots covering the tree are called *candles* because they are similar to the candles that decorate Christmas trees. At first the candles are negatively geotropic, but then they lose their geotropic response and go through elaborate movements so that they end up

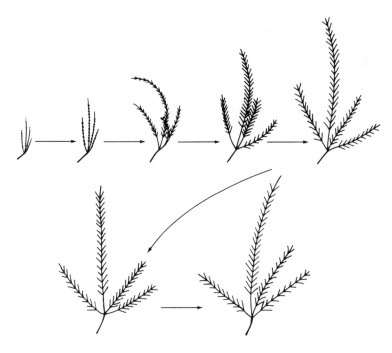

27 MOVEMENT OF PINE CANDLES
Drawings, done at weekly intervals, are of elongating shoots at the end of a lateral branch.

growing at approximately the original insertion angle (fig. 27). Some candles that were originally growing vertically upward end by growing nearly vertically downward.

Lateral buds are inserted all around the parent axis in pairs or a spiral. Therefore second-order branches off the main vertical stem grow out in different directions around the stem, but at a fairly constant angle to vertical. The slower-growing, higher-order shoots of each year tend to have a larger insertion angle and often grow out at nearly right angles. Third-order branches are inserted around each second-order branch so when they grow out some are growing upward, some nearly horizontally, and some downward. Over the years, in hardwoods like maples with bowl-shaped crowns, there is a gradual tendency for all the shoots to bend upward because of the positive geotropic tendency of the new growth, even shoots that initially grow downward. A result of this tendency is that the major branches curve up until eventually the tips of the branches are growing nearly vertically.

If the shoot above the lateral buds is cut off, then the elongating shoots from the buds bend to grow in the same general direction as the parent shoot to form replacement shoots. Their curvature is not just due to simple geotropism, because the replacement shoots bend toward the direction of the parent axis, which may be vertical for the main stem or horizontal for some higher-order branches. When the terminal is active and healthy the laterals are under apical control and grow out at their insertion angle. Without the terminal, the replacement shoot bends to less than the insertion angle. This apical control over branch angle can be replaced by putting auxin on the stub where the terminal has been cut.[1] When this is done, the elongation of the buds is reduced and they grow out at a wide angle to the parent shoot.

Some species have laterals that act like replacement shoots each year. In flowering dogwood, for instance, the terminal bud at the end of each lateral grows less than the lateral buds, particularly the lateral growing from the underside of the branch. This dominant lateral bends up and replaces the true terminal, even though the terminal may still be alive. Thus, the main axis of the branch is composed of a series of replacement branches. Such a growth pattern is more common in tropical trees.[2]

Epicormic shoots from inhibited buds grow out of the stem after injuries such as cutting, burning, or excessive pruning. Stump sprouts are really just epicormic shoots that develop at the base of a tree. Epicormic shoots are similar to replacement shoots except they often bend to grow straight up rather than in the direction of the parent axis. This vertical growth is particularly noticeable in the shoots that develop on apple trees that have been heavily pruned. These epicormic shoots do not grow out at a particular angle to their parent axis. They orient just from negative geotropism.

It is evident from these examples that some shoots have a geotropic response that is toward vertical and others have a response toward some angle away from vertical. Main stems and epicormic shoots grow directly upward. The tips of some lateral branches bend toward vertical, but then sag back down. The tips of other laterals grow out in the same direction that the branch had been growing. Replacement shoots bend to grow in the same direction as the parent even though without the injury they would have grown off at an angle. Each shoot appears to have a preferred angle. Yet that preferred angle is under apical control because when the terminal is removed the angle changes. There is one famous case in araucaria trees where branches do not change preferred angle when the terminal is injured so that branches do not bend to form replacement shoots. It is not known what determines the preferred angle or how the preferred angle can change, but it must be related to differential distribution of growth regulators.

Most trees have two options for forming replacement shoots; they either bend up existing shoots or release inhibited buds to permit vertical growth of epicormic shoots. When trees are partially tipped over by the wind, existing shoots bend to grow upward and no epicormic shoots form. If the tree is blown down, however, apical dominance and control are lost, even though the shoot system is intact, and a series of epicormic shoots grows vertically out of the horizontal stem. Branches grow more slowly and presumably produce lower concentrations of growth regulators when they are out of their preferred angle. Trees blown to the ground may grow so slowly that they lose apical dominance and control. The interaction of apical control and preferred angles makes the whole process of branch orientation extremely complicated.

THE ROOT SYSTEM

Orientation of roots in the soil is determined solely by the direction of apical growth. Once the axis is produced it is supported and encased by the soil so that it cannot sag from self-weight or be bent from cambial activity. A complicating factor is that the elongating tips are pushing their way through the soil and encountering frequent obstacles of varying resistance. Small soil particles are simply pushed aside, but such things as rocks or other thick roots force the elongating tip to change direction. To a certain extent roots avoid obstructions in the soil by growing in old root channels (the holes left after roots have died and rotted), animal holes, and cracks in the soil, but they still maintain orientation enough to establish a consistent distribution with most roots near the top of the soil and a decreasing number with increasing depth.

It is apparent from the distribution of roots that most roots are not positively geotropic. If they were, they would be found deep in the soil rather than near the surface. The first root of the seedling is positively geotropic, but most of the 90 million or so root tips in a mature tree root system are not positively geotropic.

The following description uses the orientation of red maple roots as an example.[3] The large root tips that form the horizontal woody framework of the root system have a preferred angle slightly below horizontal. These roots actually do not grow horizontally, but tend to grow at a consistent depth in the soil. Therefore, when they grow on slopes they grow at approximately the angle of the slope. Soil usually becomes more compact with increasing depth and the preferred angle of the large tips moves up as the soil becomes more compact. This is one mechanism to keep roots growing at a consistent depth.

Lateral roots with small tips grow out of the horizontal roots at approximately right angles at intervals of three to four mm. In red maples they usually grow out on opposite sides of the root. As the large tip grows through the soil it gradually twists so that over a distance the laterals are coming out in all directions. These small tips have little or no geotropic response, they just grow in whatever direction that they started. Those that grow into favorable soil proliferate and those that grow into inhospitable areas do not grow well or even die. In most cases, the favorable areas are the upper organic layers of the soil. The new generations of laterals off the short roots are not geotropic either, so they continue the process of exploring new areas and proliferating in favorable ones. Most of the distribution of fine roots is due to apparent tropisms as described above. A good example is when roots grow up into rotting stumps or logs. The few roots that happen to grow up and are in the right place to grow into the rotting wood, proliferate there. There may also be a geotropic component. Walter Lyford has painstakingly followed the longer, fine laterals in red oak.[4] He found that they gradually curved upward to reach the organic layers.

Root tips have another mechanism to maintain direction if they are deflected by obstacles in the soil. The geotropic response keeps roots growing at their preferred angle when they are deflected up or down, but has no effect on fine roots with no preferred angle or on any roots deflected to the side. In these cases the phenomenon of exotropy tends to keep the roots growing in the same direction. Like so many aspects of plant movement, exotropy was first described by Charles Darwin.[5] Root tips that grow into an obstacle and are deflected horizontally will grow in the new direction until they reach the end of the obstacle and then as they grow they bend back toward the original direction (fig. 28). Somehow they grow as though they remember the original direction. Exotropy can completely correct small deflections, but if a tip is deflected more than about forty-five degrees, the correction will be only partial and the root will grow off at a new direction. Long sections of ropelike root may appear to be

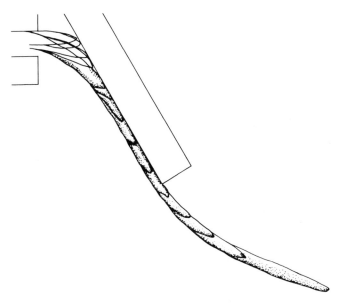

28 EXOTROPY
An aerial view sequence of a growing root tip deflected horizontally by
a barrier.

straight, but actually may have many small bends where the tip
has bent back after hitting various obstacles.

Phototropism is not important in tree root development although most roots are presumably negatively phototropic, bending away from the light. Most roots growing in the soil never are
in the light. If a root tip grows up into the surface litter during
a wet period it is more likely to be killed by subsequent dry
periods or high surface temperatures than to have a chance to utilize its phototropic response. Aerial roots from tropical trees do
grow in the light, but they generally hang down and cannot really
respond to phototropism.

Just as in shoots, when a root tip is injured the lateral roots just behind the injury bend from their usual orientation at right angles toward the direction of the parent shoot. The mechanism of this apical control in roots has not been studied. Root tips do not produce much, if any, auxin, so the mechanisms are presumably different in roots than in shoots even though the result is the same.

10 : Orientation and movement from cambial activity

THE INITIAL ORIENTATION of a shoot is established by primary growth, but the orientation can be changed later. Although the emphasis of this chapter will be on reorientation of a woody stem or branch from active bending, it is important to realize that when a woody shoot bends, all the higher order branches off the shoot are passively reoriented. The same thing happens if a shoot is tipped or broken. The most dramatic example is when a tree is tipped over by a storm. Then the stem and each branch in the crown is reoriented. Another example is when a branch bends up at the base. The outer parts of the branch, and all higher order branches along with it, rotate around the branch base. The further a shoot is from the bending base the more it is moved, even though the shoot itself does not bend at all.

A shoot can be bent by external forces like wind, snow, rain, and self-weight or by internal forces generated by differentiating wood cells. The amount of bending of an axis is determined by the amount of force acting on it and by its resistance to bending. If a shoot bends too far, it breaks. If a bending main stem puts too much stress on the roots that hold the stem in the ground then the roots break and the stem tips over.

Resistance to bending is a function of the stiffness of the wood and the cross-sectional radius of the shoot axis (fig. 29). Stiffness varies between species. Generally hardwoods like oak are stiffer than softwoods like pine. If an oak and a pine branch of the same size are bent with the same force, the pine bends more than the oak. For each species, a thicker branch bends less with a given

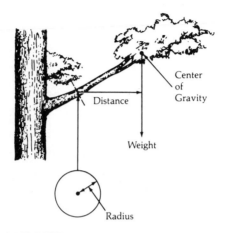

29 BRANCH BENDING
Factors determining bending force and resistance to bending in a branch.

force than a thinner branch. The stiffness of wood within an individual tree does vary with the age of the wood and the percentage of latewood, but the major variable in resistance to bending within a particular tree is the radius of the shoot. Resistance to bending of a branch that is circular in cross section is a function of the fourth power of the radius. Therefore, small growth in the radius produces big increases in stiffness. For example, if the radius increases from two to three, a 50 percent increase, the stiffness increases 500 percent, from sixteen to eighty-one. Thus, as a stem or branch thickens from cambial activity it gets much stiffer and much harder to bend.

The actual force acting to bend a shoot at any particular cross section is called the *bending moment*. The bending moment is the force acting multiplied by the distance from its plane of action (see fig. 29). To appreciate the effect of distance, hold a moderately heavy weight in your hand with your hand near your shoulder and then move your hand out until your arm is extended. As the weight moves further from your shoulder, the bending moment increases and it is harder and harder to hold the weight. For bending by self-weight the distance is measured to the center of gravity of the weight beyond the cross section. For bending by wind the distance is measured to the center of where the force is applied, essentially to the center of the sail-like structure created by the crown or branch.

Bending moments can also be generated by internal growth stresses. Growth stresses develop when fusiform wood cells tend to lengthen or shorten as the thick secondary walls differentiate. These stresses are normal by-products of cell-wall differentiation. Most cells tend to shrink as they differentiate (fig. 30), so they develop tensile stresses.[1] Each sheath of new wood that is added to the tree tends to shrink longitudinally. This tendency to shrink, and the resulting tensile stress, is resisted by the older core of wood. As more and more sheaths of wood are added in tensile stress the central core is actually compressed. In extreme cases the core is compressed so much that there are many compression failures in the wood. Eucalypts in Australia develop brittle heart in the center where the wood has so many compression failures that large beams can break under light loads because of the internal failures. Many tropical trees develop such high growth stresses that when the tree is cut the trunk splits apart. Loggers cutting such trees are in danger because if a tall tree splits up the trunk as it is being cut, the split half may suddenly move out a meter or more and kill anyone in the way.

If growth stresses are evenly distributed around the trunk then no bending force develops, but if there is an uneven distribution of stresses then there is a bending force. The bending moment is the difference in force between the opposite sides of the stem multiplied by the distance of the sheath from the center of the stem. More precisely, the distance is from the neutral plane of bending. When a branch bends, one side gets longer and the other side gets shorter. Near the center is a plane where no change in length occurs, called the *neutral plane of bending*.

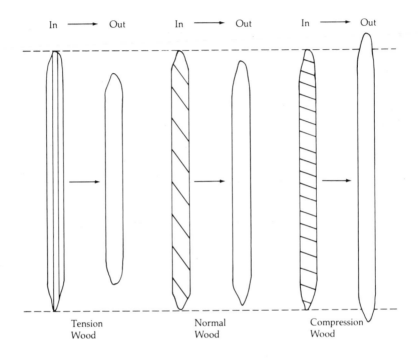

In → Out   In → Out   In → Out

Tension   Normal   Compression
Wood   Wood   Wood

30 WOOD GROWTH STRAINS
Diagrams of the change in length of wood cells when the growth stresses
are released by taking the cells out of the wood. The orientation of the
microfibrils is shown in the "in" drawing.

After a tree stem is tilted over by the wind, new wood cells
change their secondary wall differentiation to produce different
levels of growth stresses. The upper side produces wood with
higher tensile stress (it tries to shrink) and the lower side produces wood with lower tensile stress or even with compressive
stress (it tries to expand). The result is an uneven distribution of
growth stresses that tend to bend the stem toward vertical.

This tendency to produce differential growth stresses reaches
its maximum expression when reaction wood is formed. In softwoods, like pines, the underside of a leaning stem develops com-

pression wood. Compression wood cells have extra thick walls and are dark because they have a high lignin content. These compression wood cells actually develop compressive growth stresses. Because they are on the underside of the stem they act to bend it up by pushing. In hardwoods, like oak or maple, the upper side of a leaning stem develops tension wood. The tension wood cells have an extra cell wall layer and they develop very high tensile stresses, much greater than in cells with normal walls. Therefore, in hardwoods the tension wood tends to pull the branch up. The action is opposite to compression wood action in softwoods, but they both tend to bend leaning stems upward because the tension wood forms on the top and pulls, while the compression wood forms on the bottom and pushes. (Compression wood forms only in softwoods and tension wood only in hardwoods. Normal cells of both types develop tensile growth stresses.)

Reaction wood, to a large extent, is just a specialized version of normal wood that produces unusual levels of stress.[2] The exception to that conclusion is the special layer of cell wall that develops in tension wood and which is limited to tension wood cells. There seem to be two types of mechanisms responsible for growth stresses. The first mechanism is responsible for development of stresses in most cell walls (see fig. 30). Cell walls of wood are formed by cellulose strands, called *microfibrils*, that form a framework on which lignin is deposited. As the lignin is deposited it swells and pushes the microfibrils apart. The microfibrils are oriented in regular helices around the cell and the angle of the helix to the axis of the cell is critical to the amount and type of stress that develops. In normal cell walls, the angle of the microfibrils to the axis of the cells is small. As the lignin forces the microfibrils apart the cell tends to shrink and therefore develops tensile stress. The microfibril angle of cells is smallest on the upper side of leaning trees so the tensile stress is greatest. On the sides of a leaning tree the microfibril angle is almost unchanged so the tensile stress is about the same as in normal wood. On the underside, the angle is even greater and the tension is reduced even further. In conifers, the microfibril angle can increase so much that as the lignin pushes the microfibrils apart the cell actually tends to increase in length and a compressive stress develops. Compression wood is in this sense just an extension of normal wood with a larger microfibril angle and more lignin. The high lignin content in compression wood presumably increases the tendency to push the microfibrils apart and produces even higher compressive stresses. The second mechanism appears to be peculiar to the special layer of tension wood cells. This layer does not have much lignin, although other compounds are deposited on the cellulose framework. The cellulose microfibrils are oriented nearly parallel to the axis of the cells. It seems likely that in this layer the tension is generated because the cellulose microfibrils actually shrink as they are formed. The outer layers of tension wood cells behave like normal wood cell walls and the stress they develop is determined by the microfibril angle; only the extra inside layer is special.

Reaction wood forms under several different circumstances. Each stem and branch has an angle, the preferred angle, at which it does not form reaction wood. If the stem or branch is moved out of this angle it forms reaction wood to bend the axis back to the preferred angle. For example, if a vertical stem is tipped over by a wind storm it develops reaction wood to bend it back to vertical. Softwoods develop compression wood on the underside and hardwoods develop tension wood on the upperside. Horizontal branches tend to sag under their own weight so they form reaction wood to bend them back toward the horizontal. If branches are artificially bent up and tied in position they form reaction wood to force them back down to horizontal. In this example the "normal" positions are reversed, hardwoods make tension wood on the underside and softwoods make compression wood on the upperside. This induction of reaction wood because of changed orientation presumably is a response to gravitational stimulus. Somehow each axis can detect when it is out of its preferred orientation to gravity.

Reaction wood can also be induced in branches without any change in orientation, or gravitational stimulus, by removing apical control. Injuring the terminal causes reaction wood to form that will bend the branch to the orientation of the parent axis so that the branch becomes a replacement shoot.[3] Apical control can be removed by cutting off the stem above the branch or by removing a strip of bark and phloem all the way around the stem above the branch. Many branches do form some reaction wood even though they are under apical control. Generally they do not form enough reaction wood to counterbalance the downward-bending moment from the self-weight of the branch. These branches form more reaction wood when apical control is removed and the branch bends up. A few species, like ash, do not normally form reaction wood in branches, but when apical control is removed ash does form tension wood and the branch bends up. Essentially, when apical control is removed, the preferred angle of the branch changes to the angle of the parent axis and it forms reaction wood to bend to its new preferred angle.

Reaction wood formation seems to be regulated by auxin. When a stem is tipped over there is a higher auxin concentration on the underside than on the upperside. Moving the stem out of its preferred angle stimulates some mechanism, perhaps lateral auxin transport from one side of the stem to the other, that leads to differential auxin distribution. In softwoods the high concentration on the underside stimulates compression wood formation and in hardwoods the low concentration on the upperside stimulates tension wood formation. This difference in response to auxin concentration can also be shown in vertical stems that do not normally form reaction wood. If auxin is added to such a softwood stem it forms compression wood below the point of application. If auxin is reduced in a hardwood stem by adding triiodo-

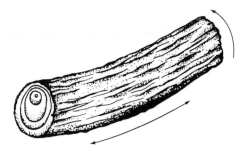

Compression wood

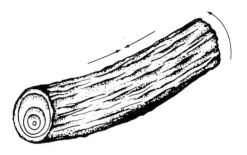

Tension wood

31   REACTION WOOD
Location and action of the two types of reaction wood in tilted stems.

benzoic acid, which stops auxin movement down the stem from the leaves, then the stem below forms tension wood.

Thus, if a vertical stem is tipped, auxin concentration is reduced on the upperside and increased on the underside. As a result, the microfibril angle of the wood produced after tipping changes and reaction wood is formed. Compression wood forms on the underside in softwoods and tension wood forms on the upperside in hardwoods (fig. 31). Compression wood tends to expand and tension wood tends to contract so both of them act to bend the stem up toward vertical. Compression wood pushes it up and tension wood pulls it up.

Reaction wood formation is usually associated with increased ring width. In a tipped stem the widest part of the ring is usually on the side where the reaction wood forms so that if it forms for some time the stem becomes eccentric with growth mostly on the top in hardwoods and on the bottom in softwoods. This correlation of increased ring width with reaction-wood formation is characteristic, but it does not always happen. The fact that reaction-wood formation and increased ring width can be separated shows that they are not controlled by the same regulators. In any case, it seems unlikely that high auxin would increase growth in softwoods and decrease it in hardwoods. It is probable that some other regulator is responsible for increasing ring width, perhaps gibberellin, but it is not clear why the regulator concentration might be higher on the top of tipped hardwood stems and on the bottom of tipped softwood stems.

When apical control is removed, a branch responds by growing faster all around, but the growth increase is greatest on the side where reaction wood forms. The location of the major increase in growth is presumably due to the same mechanism responsible for increased ring width where reaction wood forms in tipped stems. The explanation for the general increase seems to be that when the branch is under apical control most of the photosynthate it produces moves out of the branch and is used in stem growth. Essentially the branch and the stem compete for the branch photosynthate and the success of the stem in the competition depends on regulators moving down the stem from above. The most important regulator seems to be auxin because auxin can replace apical control and keep the branch from growing faster. When apical control is removed by cutting off the stem above the branch, then the branch can retain more of its photosynthate and grow more because the stem cannot compete successfully with the branch.

The angles of old branches reflect the balance between bending down by self-weight and bending up by reaction wood. Many softwoods that have a central stem much larger than the branches, like pines, show a clear sequence of branch angles from the young branches at the top to the older branches at the bottom. Young branches grow at about a forty-five-degree angle. As the branches elongate, most of the photosynthate either goes into making more needles and elongating the branch or is transported out of the branch to the stem. There is some cambial activity to thicken the branch, but not enough to keep it from sagging from the increased bending moment of its own weight. Toward the tip the branch usually bends up slightly because the tip elongates somewhat upward and it takes several years of loading from increased branch weight before the old tip portion is bent down. Therefore, at the bottom of a pine tree the branches are near horizontal except toward the tip. In a maple grown in the open, however, the main stem is quite short and there are many large branches. The lower branches grow rapidly and sweep up until the tips are nearly vertical. Enough photosynthate is retained by the branches so that they thicken and are not bent down very much by the increasing self-weight.

TREES IN MOST regions need to survive occasional hard times. For a large part of the world, the hard times are the cold winters. In other parts there are droughts (although trees do not grow at all in the driest parts of the world) and floods. Most of these hard times occur annually at fairly regular seasons. Trees usually start preparations before the hard times actually arrive. If a tree were still growing when there was a freeze it might be killed, so there is a tremendous advantage for it to be dormant and frost-hardy well before the dangers of winter arrive. To prepare ahead of time trees have to use environmental cues. Trees, like most organisms, are sensitive to day length. They can essentially tell what time of year it is by the length of the day. Many of the preparations for winter start as the days begin to get shorter in the summer. If days are extended with artificial light, the trees just keep on growing as if it were early summer.

Along rivers, trees are flooded regularly, usually in the spring before the leaves grow out and when the trees are most resistant to flooding. Trees that are regularly flooded for long periods have special mechanisms to survive the problem of insufficient root aeration.[1] Other trees are killed by extended flooding when they are in leaf.

Droughts that are not seasonal cannot be cued by day length, but they develop slowly as the soil dries out, so the decreased water availability is another kind of environmental cue. When the water potential in the leaf drops, the leaf begins to form abscisic acid. The abscisic acid stimulates the stomata to close. Abscisic acid that forms under water stress acts as an early warning system so that the tree stops water loss before water stress gets so severe that there is serious damage. Where droughts are seasonal, trees may use photoperiod as a cue and set buds and shed leaves before the drought season arrives. Trees that live in very dry areas have many special adaptations to reduce transpiration and to withstand the high temperatures usually associated with arid areas of the world.

Preparation for winter is a long complex process. In many trees, buds begin to form in early summer, but the actual formation of the buds may take a month or more as the bud scales and early leaves are produced. The buds are small as they are forming and usually are hidden by leaf bases. The first easily visible signs of preparation for winter are associated with leaf senescence. Each leaf passes through a life cycle. First it is produced by the meristem. It may then spend a winter inside a bud, but it eventually grows out to form a stalk and a blade. Once growth stops, senescence begins as the leaf ages. Leaves on evergreen trees may live more than a year, but they also age and eventually die. For deciduous trees, as autumn approaches the green chlorophyll pigment in the leaves begins to break down and other yellow, red, and brown pigments which had been masked by the chlorophyll produce the colors of autumn foliage. Some species produce more red pigments as fall approaches. Photoperiod is the major signal for the beginning of autumn color changes, although the speed of development may be hastened by cold weather. Just what determines whether the autumn colors will be brilliant and "good" or pale and washed out is a wonderful subject for argument. No one is really sure what the answer is, whether it is best to have wet or dry summers, or hot or cold springs; therefore the argument continues and everybody has a chance of having his or her pet hypothesis be at least partially correct.

The final stage of the leaf life cycle for most leaves is leaf fall, or leaf abscission.[2] Most leaves do not simply fall off. They break off through a special abscission zone at the base of the leaf stalk. The abscission zone is not present in the summer. In the autumn, as the growth-regulator production by the leaf blade begins to decrease, the zone forms. There are localized cell divisions to form the zone and then the cells in the zone actually begin to separate from each other. As this process continues, the action of the leaf blowing in the wind, or just its own weight, completes the separation between the cells, and the leaf falls. The timing of leaf fall is dependent on the timing of the formation of the abscission zone. Some oaks do not form abscission zones and their leaves eventually are broken off by wind action.

Not only leaves form abscission zones. The needle bundles on pines, for example, are actually tiny short shoots with a stem only a millimeter or so long. When pine needles fall, actually the whole short shoot falls and the abscission zone forms at the base of the short shoot. Some species shed whole small branch units. There is a large group of tree species that actually sheds the terminal portion of each shoot each year, well before leaf fall. In all cases the abscission permits a clean break and the exposed cells of the abscission layer are specially modified to protect the self-imposed wound from attack by insects and decay organisms.

Early in the summer, buds are not dormant, they are inhibited. During this period some buds may start to grow (for example lammas growth and multiple flush) under good weather conditions or if the stem or leaves are injured. As autumn approaches the buds gradually become dormant. Inhibitors build up in the buds so they will not grow no matter what the weather or if the stem and leaves are injured. Dormant buds have a chilling requirement before they can grow again. That requirement is met by temperatures around freezing. Different species have different length chilling requirements ranging from a few weeks to a few months.

Bud dormancy and leaf abscission are not enough preparation

to survive a winter. Shortening photoperiods cue the tree to develop dormant buds and lose their leaves, but it is the first cold days of autumn that are the environmental cue for trees to develop resistance to below-freezing temperatures. When trees are growing, the cells cannot stand below-freezing temperatures because ice crystals forming inside the cells tear membranes and kill the cells. Frost-hardy trees can stand very low temperatures because no large ice crystals form in the cells. Frost hardiness is developed in each individual cell, it is not stimulated by some regulator transmitted from leaves. As the cells become frost-hardy their water content is reduced and the structure of the cell's contents changes. The result is that the water is in such small, separate compartments that it can be supercooled to temperatures well below freezing without forming ice crystals. If the water in the cell does freeze it forms tiny ice crystals that do not hurt the membrane. Larger ice crystals may form in the spaces between cells where they do no damage. When these intercellular ice crystals begin to form they actually draw water from the inside of the cells, further reducing the cell's water content. Thus, frost-hardy cells still cannot tolerate ice-crystal formation, but they have changed to avoid the problem so that no dangerous ice crystals are formed within them.

Another aspect of preparation for winter is the storage of photosynthate for growth the next spring. Deciduous trees in the spring must grow on stored photosynthate until the leaves become self-sufficient. Evergreen trees can use old leaves for photosynthesis early in the season, but they also need stored photosynthate for the rapid shoot growth of spring. Photosynthate is stored mostly as starch. Storage may be in parenchyma cells in the roots, stems, or, for evergreen species, leaves. Most of the material for early growth is stored in the twigs for deciduous species and in old leaves for evergreens. A great deal of starch may be stored in roots. Tree pathologists sometimes use the amount of stored root starch as an indicator of tree vigor.[3] In fast-growing poplar trees the root starch is mobilized and used in early growth. In some species root starch may stay almost constant throughout the year.

Occasionally there are springlike periods during a long cold winter. Trees do not start growing during these warm spells. They have two safeguards. One is photoperiod. Trees have a mechanism that will not permit growth until day length is longer than some critical length. The other is a requirement for a certain number of warm days before the trees will start to grow. We can express the extent of this requirement in some measurement like growing-degree days. A growing-degree day is a day whose average temperature is greater than 6 c (43 f). White spruce trees growing in Massachusetts and white spruce trees growing in Alaska all started growing in the spring after eleven growing-degree days even though day lengths are quite different.[4] The warm days do not have to come all at once; they can accumulate. Such a control suggests that in warm weather some sequence of reactions occurs that finally leads to growth. The reactions occur above some minimum temperature, but do not vary much with temperature when they are in progress.

Breaking of bud dormancy seems to occur because of the balance between inhibitors and promoters. During the chilling period either inhibitors decrease or the promoters, gibberellin and cytokinin, increase. In many plants, dormant buds can be made to grow by bringing them indoors and treating them with gibberellin. A possible source of gibberellin in the spring is from the roots. Usually roots start to grow before the buds do. The growing roots produce gibberellin, which can then move up into the shoot system and start shoot growth. Like most processes controlled by growth regulators, dormancy and the breaking of dormancy seem to involve several different regulators in a complex interaction.

Another way for a tree to survive hard times is as a seed. A seed is actually a whole little tree inside protective seed coats. Seeds of mangroves actually germinate on the tree and fall as a partially grown little plant. Some seeds will germinate and grow as soon as they reach the ground and get enough moisture. In temperate areas these seed are usually shed in early summer so that the seedling has a season for growth. In the eastern United States the red maple is a good example of a plant that flowers early in the spring, rapidly develops seed, and sheds them. Most of the seed germinate within a few days under moist conditions, although a few may not germinate until the next year.

It is more common, in temperate areas, for seeds to be shed in the fall. These seed are usually dormant, they will not germinate even with adequate moisture and warm temperatures. Just like dormant buds, the dormant seed usually require a period of cold temperature before they will germinate. Seeds are very resistant to inhospitable environments. They permit the little tree inside simply to avoid the bad times and not grow until the environment is favorable. The seed of most species will grow in the spring after their chilling requirement has been met, but some will stay dormant in the soil for many years. One of the best examples is the pin cherry which often forms a dense thicket of trees after clear cuts or major storm damage. Seeds of pin cherry are carried by birds and dropped onto the forest floor. They soon become buried by leaf litter. The seeds can stay dormant for ninety or more years, until a large opening is created that stimulates germination. The stimulus for germination appears to be the increased soil temperature and soil nitrate from litter breakdown when the sun reaches the surface after the forest has been removed. Thus, pin cherry (and raspberry too) can occupy openings rapidly because, in fact, the trees were already there. They were lying hidden and dormant as seeds in the soil.

There are many different mechanisms for seed dormancy. The seed coats may impose dormancy. In these cases the little plant inside the seed will grow if the seed coats are removed. The seed coats may physically keep the seed from germinating by restricting water or gas exchange, or by being too strong to be broken. The seed coats may also produce inhibitors that keep the seed dormant. Many seeds will not germinate even though the seed coats are removed. In a few cases the little plant, the embryo, is not sufficiently developed to germinate, in other cases the embryo itself produces inhibitors that keep it from growing.

When seeds are dormant because of inhibitors, they undergo changes in the balance of inhibitors and promoters during the chilling period. These changes are similar to those that occur within dormant buds during the chilling period. Dormant seed will often germinate without cold treatment if treated with gibberellin or cytokinin. Some species respond to one promoter and some to the other. Striped maple seed need three months of moist, cold temperature before they will germinate. Removing the seed coats does not speed germination, but when the seed without seed coats are treated with cytokinin they germinate within four days.

When the seed germinates the tree starts to grow. The various processes described in preceding chapters take place year after year. New parts are added to the shoot and root systems. Some axes thicken and some die as the bulk of the tree is built up. If the tree is successful the photosynthetic machinery in the leaves gets enough light and other growth factors from the environment to produce materials for further growth. The different roots and shoots interact with each other to produce the characteristic patterns and form that we associate with each species. Eventually the tree produces seeds itself, the cycle goes on, and the species survives.

References

1 : What Is a Tree and How Does It Grow?

1   Ward, H. M. 1909. *Trees*. Vol. 5. *Form and Habit*. Cambridge University Press, Cambridge.

2   Forrester, J. W. 1968. *Principles of Systems*. Wright-Allen Press, Cambridge, Massachusetts. (The same modeling technique that works for trees was used to model the world population in Meadows, D. H.; D. L. Meadows; and W. D. Behrens III. 1972. *The Limits to Growth*. Universe Books, New York.)

3   Harper, J. L. 1977. *Population Biology of Plants*. Academic Press, New York. See p. 29.

4   Allen, G. S., and N. J. Owens. 1972. *The Life History of Douglas-Fir*. Canada Forest Service. (For general treatments consult Kozlowski, T. T. 1971. *Growth and Development of Trees*. Vols. 1 and 2. Academic Press, New York; and Kramer, P. J. and T. T. Kozlowski. 1979. *Physiology of Woody Plants*. Academic Press, New York.

2 : Tree Design

1   Hallé, F.; R. A. A. Oldeman; and P. B. Tomlinson. 1978. *Tropical Trees and Forests: An Architectural Analysis*. Springer, New York.

2   Barghoorn, E. S. 1964. "Evolution of cambium in geologic time." In *The Formation of Wood in Forest Trees* (M. H. Zimmermann, ed.), pp. 3–17. Academic Press, New York.

3   Horn, H. 1971. *The Adaptive Geometry of Trees*. Princeton University Press, Princeton.

4   Borchert, R. 1973. "Simulation of rhythmic tree growth under constant conditions." *Physiologia Plantarum* 35:152–57.

5   Bailey, I. W. 1954. "Contributions to plant anatomy." *Chronica Botanica* 15: 127–38 (article reprinted from 1944 *Amer. J. Bot.* 31:421–28).

6 Zimmermann, M. H., and C. L. Brown. 1971. *Trees: Structure and Function.* Springer, New York. Chapter 4.

7 Harper, J. L. 1977. *Population Biology of Plants.* Academic Press, New York. Chapters 19, 20.

3 : Additive and Multiplicative Growth

1 Bailey, I. W. 1954. "Contributions to plant anatomy." *Chronica Botanica* 15: 21–29 (article reprinted from 1923 *Amer. J. Bot.* 10:499–509).

2 Bannan, M. W. 1957. "The relative frequency of the different types of anticlinal divisions in conifers." *Canad. J. Bot.* 35:875–84; and Bannan, M. W. 1965. "Ray contacts and the rate of anticlinal division in fusiform cambial cells of some *Pinaceae.*" *Canad. J. Bot.* 43:487–507.

4 : Pattern and Form

1 Hallé, F.; R. A. A. Oldeman; and P. B. Tomlinson. 1978. *Tropical Trees and Forests: An Architectural Analysis.* Springer, New York. (See the concept of reiteration.)

2 Brunig, E. F. 1976. "Tree forms in relation to environmental conditions: an ecological viewpoint." In *Tree Physiology and Yield Improvement* (M. G. R. Cannell and F. T. Last, eds.), pp. 139–56. Academic Press, New York.

3 Ewers, F. W., and R. Schmid. 1981. "Longevity of needle fascicles of *Pinus longaeva* (bristlecone pine) and other North American pines." *Oecologia* 51: 107–15.

4 Horn, H. S. 1971. *The Adaptive Geometry of Trees.* Princeton University Press, Princeton.

5 See Hallé, Oldeman, and Tomlinson, *Tropical Trees and Forests.*

6 Honda, H., and J. B. Fisher. 1978. "Tree branch angle: maximizing effective leaf area." *Science* 199:888–90.

7 Givnish, T. J. 1978. "On the adaptive significance of compound leaves, with particular reference to tropical trees." In *Tropical Trees as Living Systems* (P. B. Tomlinson and M. H. Zimmermann, eds.), pp. 351–80. Cambridge University Press, New York. See also Corner, E. J. H. 1964. *The Life of Plants.* New American Library, New York.

8 Vogt, K. A.; R. I. Edmonds; and C. Grier. 1981. "Seasonal changes in biomass and vertical distribution of mycorrhizal and fibrous-textured conifer

fine roots in 23- and 180-year-old subalpine *Abies amabilis* stands." *Canad. J. Forest Res.* 11:223–29.

9   Lyford, W. H. 1980. "Development of the root system of northern red oak (*Quercus rubra* L.)." *Harvard Forest Paper* No. 21:1–30.

10 Harley, J. L., and S. E. Smith. 1983. *Mycorrhizal Symbiosis.* Academic Press, New York. See also Akinson, D.; K. K. S. Bhat; M. P. Coutts; P. A. Mason; and D. J. Read. 1983. *Tree Root Systems and Their Mycorrhizas.* Nijhoff/Junk, The Hague, Netherlands.

5 : Regulation of Growth

1   Zimmermann, M. H., and C. L. Brown. 1971. *Trees: Structure and Function.* Springer, New York.

2   Gill, C. J. 1970. "The flooding tolerance of woody species—a review." *Forestry Abstracts* 31:671–88.

3   There is no comprehensive review of growth regulators in trees—it is too big a field—but for an introduction see: Kramer, P. J., and T. T. Kozlowski. 1979. *Physiology of Woody Plants.* Academic Press, New York.

4   See Zimmermann and Brown, *Trees: Structure and Function.*

5   Green, P. B. 1980. "Organogenesis—a biophysical view." *Annual Rev. Plant Physiol.* 31:51–82.

6   Brown, C. L. 1964. "The influence of external pressure on the differentiation of cells and tissues cultured in vitro." In *Formation of Wood in Forest Trees* (M. H. Zimmermann, ed.), pp. 389–404. Academic Press, New York.

6 : Elongation and Leaf Production

1   Little, C. H. A. 1970. "Apical dominance in long shoots of white pine (*Pinus strobus*)." *Canad. J. Bot.* 48:239–53.

2   Powell, G. R.; K. I. Tosh; and J. E. MacDonald. 1982. "Indeterminate shoot extension and heterophylly in *Acer saccharum.*" *Canad. J. Forest Res.* 12:166–70.

3   Lyr, H., and G. Hoffman. 1967. "Growth rates and growth periodicity of tree roots." *Int. Rev. Forestry Res.* 2:191–236.

4   Borchert, R. 1973. "Simulation of rhythmic tree growth under constant conditions." *Physiologia Plantarum* 35:152–57.

7 : Formation and Fate of Apical Meristems

1   Torrey, J. G. 1965. "Physiological bases for organization and development in the root." *Encyclopedia of Plant Physiology* 15/1:1256–1327 (see esp. 1310–17).

2   See the following chapters in Torrey, J. G., and D. T. Clarkson, eds. 1975. *The Development and Function of Roots*. Academic Press, New York: Dart, P. J. "Legume root nodule initiation and development," pp. 467–506; Becking, J. H. "Root nodules in non-legumes," pp. 507–66; and Gerdemann, J. W. "Vescicular-arbuscular mycorrhizae," pp. 575–91.

8 : Thickening from Cambial Activity

1   Duff, G. H., and N. J. Nolan. 1953. "Growth and morphogenesis in the Canadian forest species. 1. The control of cambial and apical activity in *Pinus resinosa* Ait." *Canad. J. Bot.* 31:471–513. (Other titles in a series of papers are cited in D. Forward and N. J. Nolan. 1964. *Canad. J. Bot.* 42:923–50.)

2   Wilson, B. F. 1975. "Distribution of secondary thickening in tree root systems." In *The Development and Function of Plant Roots* (J. G. Torrey and D. T. Clarkson, eds.), pp. 197–219. Academic Press, New York.

3   Digby, J., and P. F. Wareing. 1966. "The effect of applied growth hormones on cambial division and the differentiation of cambial derivatives." *Ann. Bot.* 119:539–48.

4   Digby, J., and P. F. Wareing. 1966. "The relationship between endogenous hormone levels in the plant and seasonal aspects of cambial activity." *Ann. Bot.* 120:607–22.

5   Gregory, R. A., and B. F. Wilson. 1968. "A comparison of cambial activity of white spruce in Alaska and New England." *Canad. J. Bot.* 46:733–34.

6   Wilson, B. F., and R. R. Archer. 1979. "Tree design: some biological solutions to mechanical problems." *BioScience* 29:293–98.

7   Jacobs, M. R. 1939. "A study of the effect of sway on trees." *Commonwealth Forestry Bureau Bull.* (Australia) 26:1–17.

8   Kennedy, R. W. 1961. "Variation and periodicity of summerwood in some second-growth Douglas-fir." *Tappi* 44:161–66.

9   Larson, P. R. 1964. "Some indirect effects of environment on wood formation." In *Formation of Wood in Forest Trees* (M. H. Zimmermann, ed.), pp. 345–65. Academic Press, New York.

10 Wodzicki, T. J. 1978. "Seasonal variation of auxin in cambial region of *Pinus silvestris* L." *Acta Soc. Bot. Poloniae* 47:225–31.

11 Denne, M. P., and R. S. Dodd. 1981. "The environmental control of xylem differentiation." In *Xylem Cell Development* (J. R. Barnett, ed.), pp. 236–55. Castle House, Tunbridge Wells, England.

12 Doley, D., and L. Leyton. 1968. "Effects of growth regulating substances and water potential on the development of secondary xylem in *Fraxinus.*" *New Phytol.* 67:579–94.

13 Vité, J. P., and J. A. Rudinsky. 1959. "The water conducting systems in conifers and their importance to the distribution of trunk injected chemicals." *Contrib. Boyce Thompson Inst.* 20:27–38.

14 Harris, J. M. 1981. "Spiral grain formation." In Barnett, *Xylem Cell Development*, pp. 256–90.

9 : Orientation and Movement from Apical Growth

1 Jankiewicz, L. S. 1956. "The effect of auxins on crotch angles in apple trees." *Bull. Acad. Polonaise Sci.* Ser. 2, 4:173–78.

2 Hallé, F.; R. A. A. Oldeman; and P. B. Tomlinson. 1978. *Tropical Trees and Forests: An Architectural Analysis.* Springer, New York.

3 Lyford, W. H., and B. F. Wilson, 1964. "Development of the root system of *Acer rubrum* L." *Harvard Forest Paper* No. 10:1–17. See also Wilson, B. F. 1964. "Structure and growth of woody roots of *Acer rubrum* L." *Harvard Forest Paper* No. 11:1–14. Wilson, B. F. 1967. "Root growth around barriers." *Bot. Gazette* 128:79–82; Wilson, B. F. 1970. "Evidence for injury as a cause for tree root branching." *Canad. J. Bot.* 48:1497–98; Wilson, B. F. 1971. "Vertical orientation of red maple (*Acer rubrum* L.) roots." *Canad. J. For. Res.* 1:147–50.

4 Lyford, W. H. 1980. "Development of the root system of northern red oak (*Quercus rubra* L.)." *Harvard Forest Paper* No. 21:1–30.

5 Darwin, C. 1898. *The Power of Movement in Plants.* Appleton, New York.

10 : Orientation and Movement from Cambial Activity

1 Jacobs, M. R. 1945. "The growth stresses of woody stems." *Commonwealth Forestry Bureau Bull.* (Australia) 28:1–67.

2 Wilson, B. F. 1981. "The development of growth strains and stresses in reaction wood." In *Xylem Cell Development* (J. R. Barnett, ed.), pp. 275–90. Castle House, Tunbridge Wells, England.

3 Wilson, B. F., and R. R. Archer. 1981. "Apical control of branch movements in white pine: biological aspects." *Plant Physiol.* 68:1285–88.

11 : Survival in Hard Times

1   Etherington, J. R. 1982. *Environment and Plant Ecology*. 2d ed. John Wiley and Sons, New York. Chapter 7.

2   Addicott, F. T. 1982. *Abscission*. University of California Press, Berkeley and Los Angeles.

3   Wargo, P. M. 1975. "Estimating starch content in roots of deciduous trees—a visual technique." *USDA Forest Service Res. Paper* NE–313.

4   Gregory, R. A., and B. F. Wilson. 1968. "A comparison of cambial activity of white spruce in Alaska and New England." *Canad. J. Bot.* 46:733–34.

Scientific names of plants

Alder *Alnus* spp.
Araucaria *Araucaria* spp.
Ash *Fraxinus* spp.
Basswood *Tilia* spp.
Beech *Fagus grandifolia*
Beech, European (with many varieties)
 Fagus sylvatica
Birch *Betula* spp.
Bladdernut *Staphylea trifolia*
Casuarina *Casuarina* spp.
Cherry *Prunus* spp.
Cherry, pin *Prunus pensylvanica*
Chestnut *Castanea dentata*
Cork tree *Phellodendron amurense*
Dogwood, flowering *Cornus florida*
Douglas-fir *Pseudotsuga menziesii*
Elm *Ulmus* spp.
Elm, American *Ulmus americana*
Eucalypt *Eucalyptus* spp.
Fig *Ficus* spp.
Fig, strangling *Ficus aurea*
Fir *Abies* spp.
Gale, sweet *Myrica gale*
Hemlock *Tsuga* spp.
Locust *Gleditsia* spp., *Robinia* spp.
Maple *Acer* spp.
Maple, red *Acer rubrum*
Maple, striped *Acer pensylvanicum*
Maple, sugar *Acer saccharum*
Oak *Quercus* spp.

Oak, pin *Quercus palustris*
Oak, red *Quercus rubra*
Olive, Russian *Elaeagnus angustifolia*
Pine *Pinus* spp.
Pine, bristlecone *Pinus aristata*
Pine, red *Pinus resinosa*
Poplar *Populus* spp.
Poplar, Lombardy *Populus nigra*
 var. *italica*
Raspberry *Rubus* spp.
Redbud *Cercis canadensis*
Redwood *Sequoia sempervirens*
Spruce *Picea* spp.
Spruce, white *Picea glauca*
Sumac, staghorn *Rhus typhina*
Sweetgum *Liquidambar styraciflua*
Sycamore *Platanus occidentalis*
Willow *Salix* spp.
Willow, weeping *Salix babylonica*

Library of Congress Cataloging in Publication Data
Wilson, Brayton F. (Brayton Fuller), 1934–
The growing tree.
Includes bibliographical references and index.
1. Trees—Growth. I. Title.
SD396.W55   1984   582.16'031   84–3577
ISBN 0–87023–423–4
ISBN 0–87023–424–2 (pbk.)